EXTERNALITIES AND WELFARE

COLUMBIA STUDIES IN ECONOMICS

6

This book is based on the author's doctoral dissertation, "Generalized Joint Product Pricing—Application to Externalities and Transfer Prices," which was awarded the Harry G. Friedman prize as the best dissertation in the Economics Department at Columbia University for 1968–69.

DAVID K. WHITCOMB

EXTERNALITIES
AND WELFARE

 *Columbia University Press*
NEW YORK AND LONDON
1972

David K. Whitcomb is Assistant Professor of
Economics in the Graduate School of Business
Administration at New York University

Copyright © 1972 Columbia University Press
ISBN *0-231-03586-1*
Library of Congress Catalog Card Number: 71-172174
Printed in the United States of America

ACKNOWLEDGMENTS

A number of people have made major contributions to this work. Professor Stanislaw Wellisz of Columbia first interested me in externalities, helped me define the goals and scope of the dissertation from which this book has grown, and gave me a great deal of specific help. I could not have had a more encouraging and considerate dissertation sponsor. Professor Enrique Arzac, also of Columbia, suggested important elements of several proofs in chapters 2 and 4. Professor Sadik Gokturk of St. John's University significantly influenced the development of chapter 2 in many discussions and by the example of his own important work on joint production. His ideas were "tiny time pills," set to go off now and then over the several years I have worked on this subject. Professors Kelvin Lancaster, Donald Dewey, Carl Shoup, and William Vickrey, all of Columbia; Professor Charles Shami of Yeshiva University; and Mr. Fred Sudit of New York University read various drafts and made important and constructive suggestions, some of which are specifically acknowledged in the text. I am also grateful for the opportunity I have had to present some parts of this work in seminars at New York University and at Stanford and for the helpful comments I received.

Mr. Curtis Browne served briefly and productively as a research assistant. Miss Ruth Eifert expertly typed the final draft of the manuscript, and even after reading it, was kind enough to ask me for a copy of the book.

I am indebted to the National Science Foundation, the Ford Foundation, and the New York University Schools of Business Research Fund for financial support.

ACKNOWLEDGEMENTS

Finally, I want to thank my wife, Henrietta, for, among many things, giving me the best definition of mutual separable external economies:

> Jack Sprat could eat no fat,
> His wife could eat no lean;
> And so betwixt them both,
> They licked the platter clean.
> *Mother Goose*

D. K. W.

CONTENTS

ix

EXTERNALITIES AND WELFARE

ONE

INTRODUCTION

1.1. What and why

A recent paper by James Buchanan began: "This note is presented as a contribution to the continuing dismantling of the Pigovian tradition in applied economics defined here as the emphasis on internalizing externalities through the imposition of corrective taxes and subsidies."[1] The central purpose of this monograph is to show that however many nails have been hammered into the coffin of the Pigovian tradition, there is not yet a corpse inside. The dismantling has been useful, but it has gone far enough. It is time to start rebuilding.

Why? Why study externalities? We can justify the effort on purely welfare theoretic grounds, and maybe we should, and not search for any other reason. Welfare economics has become an essentially negative exercise, and over the past twenty years we have made considerable retrogress in its study. One of the areas of greatest retrogress is externalities. Once the new welfare economics was developed we quickly found that the presence of external economies and diseconomies was one of the major exceptions to the proposition that the invisible hand guides us to a Pareto optimum.[2] And we have gone steadily downhill from there. Most of those who have worked most closely with externalities over the past ten years seem to have come to the conclusion that Pigou's taxes and subsidies cannot work; that is, they cannot enforce Pareto optimal externality levels. Much of the recent literature has been devoted to demonstrating this conclusion, and we shall survey it in section 1.3. Some leave us there,

---

[1] Buchanan (1969), p. 174.

[2] Not that this exception was new: Marshall's and Pigou's conclusions were just reaffirmed in the models built on the "scientific" Pareto criterion.

1

hopeless. Others offer us the proposition (if you don't read them very carefully) that nonoptimal externality levels don't exist because private bargains among the parties affected have restored Pareto optimality. Look around you; it ain't so.

If the aim of welfare economics is to find the efficiency frontier (leaving to the political process the choice among points on the frontier) without eliminating decentralized decision-making, we must modify the tax/subsidy approach to make it work or replace it with a believable alternative. Either would be a start, in one area, toward making welfare economics a little less negative.

Externalities remain one of the underdeveloped areas of economics, an exception to "the principles" of price and welfare theory rather than a part of them. It would be desirable to integrate externalities into the core of modern economic theory, but presumptous to say this monograph achieves it. This is, though, one of its motivations; and it helps explain why I spend so much time on production theory and the derivation of Pareto optimality conditions. Also, we can view the Pigovian theorem as an extension of the "competition results in Pareto optimal outputs" theorem of welfare economics to say that "shadow prices" can be assigned that impel competitive firms maximizing their individual profit to produce Pareto optimal levels of externalities. And we mustn't forget the attractions of an underdeveloped area (if it is really underdeveloped and not just resource-poor). As Galbraith modestly puts it: "I have always thought it unwise to compete with the commonplace."

We can also justify the study of externalities, even theoretical study, on the grounds of potential relevance to real issues of national policy. Public interest in environment externalities, such as pollution in all its forms, is at fever pitch. However much one may regret intellectual fads, which sometimes disappear before accomplishing anything beyond raising expectations, the economics profession must respond to interest in a *legitimate* topic or be declared irrelevant. And particularly *this* topic! The profession has already had a lot to do with the way the public debate has been framed. For example, Pigou's taxes and subsidies have just lately been rediscovered (or perhaps discovered) by the politicians as an alternative to outright prohibition in some cases. (If anything pleases politicians more than prohibition of things, it is taxation of them!) Theoretical analysis has also led to the conclusion (put best by Coase [1960]) that since

2

the Pareto optimal externality level is not always zero, it is sometimes better to live with externalities or induce the resources involved to move. This is obviously relevant to such issues as the noise along airport approach paths.

There are two current policy issues to which I believe this monograph has some relevance. One is the question whether we must substantially reduce or make negative our rate of economic growth in order to reduce environmental externalities to "acceptable" levels. Obviously this would mean a change in our whole way of life. The second issue is whether a tax on the quantity of pollutants can be an effective measure, to whom it should be paid, and whether it should be the same for all producers of the pollutant. Neither of these issues is resolved by this monograph. All a theoretical work can hope to do is raise the level of the debate a little.

Now as to what I really intend to do: The first thing is to limit the scope of the endeavor to externalities among producers, by far the easiest case.[3] This is explained and justified (as far as possible) in the next section, on definition and economic setting. The inevitable review of the literature follows, in section 1.3. This has two goals: first, to reproduce as accurately as possible the main points made by the dismantlers of the Pigovian tradition; and second, to show the great restrictiveness of the "traditional" model of externalities.

The construction of an analytical framework begins with the latter point. Taking a long look at the production function of a firm producing and receiving externalities, it becomes clear that a generalized joint product formulation makes it possible to describe more realistically why an externality is produced and how its level can be altered at least cost. This may condition economists to be a little less pessimistic about the possibilities of reducing undesirable externalities without completely sacrificing economic growth. We can use this production function to derive a cost function, which it is convenient to use in the parts of the monograph concerned with tax/subsidy schemes.

We also use the production function to derive graphically and mathematically the conditions for achieving Pareto efficient output levels when production externalities are present. Graphically, an open-topped Edgeworth box is developed with tangency of isoquants required for efficiency. Mathematically, the efficiency conditions can be interpreted analogously

---

[3] Some of the results and a good deal of the technique should carry over to an analysis of externalities affecting consumers.

to Samuelson's public goods condition: the marginal rates of technical substitution between the input and the externality summed over the firms receiving the externality equals the marginal social cost of producing the externality (rate at which a valuable private good must be used to produce the externality). These efficiency conditions are not entirely without precedent in the literature, but are somewhat novel in that they use production functions rather than transformation functions. The latter do not convey the character of an externality so well and do not enable us to distinguish among firms.

The efficiency conditions derived by maximizing one saleable output holding the other saleable outputs and inputs constant are also satisfied when combined profit of the firms is maximized. The conventional rule for achieving a "social optimum" in the presence of production externalities is to maximize combined profit. The analysis described here justifies this rule in terms of the first principles of modern welfare economics. In addition, the rule "maximize combined profit" provides (an arbitrary) means of selecting one from among an infinite number of Pareto efficient points.

The Pigovian problem is to give firms incentive to produce Pareto optimal externality levels without simply ordering them to do so. We shall examine the "standard" tax/subsidy schemes and see that they do not always succeed in providing this decentralized initiative. For example, the requirement that the firm producing an external diseconomy pay damages to the firm(s) affected is ineffective when cost functions are of the "nonseparable" type Davis and Whinston (1962) have shown we must often expect. In fact, the Davis-Whinston development has cast doubt on all tax/subsidy schemes. As of now, the theoretical literature leaves the strong impression that no tax per unit of externality (such as the proposed taxes on lead and on water pollutants) can work, even with perfect information. Perhaps it is fortunate that the literature isn't widely read because the impression is wrong.

The central hypothesis of this book is that optimal taxes and subsidies can be found such that once they have been assigned by a central authority, *all conflict of interest among the relevant firms as to desired output levels is removed and the firms are stimulated to produce Pareto optimal outputs.* The uncertainty as to output levels brought about by nonseparable cost functions is eliminated. Necessary and sufficient conditions for such optimal taxes and subsidies are derived for completely general cost functions. The conditions for the important special case of strictly convex cost functions form the basis of an algorithm for determining optimal *per-unit* taxes and subsidies (generalized joint product "shadow prices").

The generalized joint product model and the shadow price algorithm also apply to the "transfer price" problem (setting prices on intermediate products transferred among divisions of a large firm so as to promote decentralization). We can prove several theorems about the shadow prices for externalities and for transferred products which have policy implications in certain contexts. (For example, the externality tax must be paid to the recipient of the externality, but if there are several recipients, each may get a different unit tax. Transfer prices must be the same if several divisions use the same intermediate product.) These theorems, taken together, constitute a proof of quantity-price duality between public and private production goods. This extends somewhat the concept of duality between public and private goods first noted by Samuelson (1955).

Under the assumption that a central authority possesses perfect information on the cost functions of the firms affected by externalities, we can now show that the shadow prices it computes are optimal. Those attacking the Pigovian tradition have usually claimed the contrary. We have accomplished one of our main purposes.

Questions as to the degree of perfection of the information reaching the central authority and the cost of administration are the *legitimate* sources of doubt about centrally computed taxes and subsidies. Decentralized approaches provide possible alternatives. The latter have not been extensively questioned in the externalities literature. We shall examine two. The Davis-Whinston (1966) *tatonnement* tax/subsidy scheme will be shown to suffer from the failure of its iterative processes to converge and from undetectable cheating. The "private bargain" approach is plagued by problems of bargaining breakdown. Both centralized and decentralized approaches have problems then. Much of the analysis here can be viewed as an attempt to correct the imbalance in the recent literature and make sure we discuss the real problems in future research.

1.2. Definition and economic setting

There is a great and star-studded literature in economics which consists of defining externalities. One might even say we spend more time defining them than doing anything about them. The most general definition which has evolved from this literature is: "A technological externality exists when some activity of party A imposes a cost or benefit on party B for which A is not charged or compensated by the price system of a market economy."

Either party may be a consumer or a firm and may consist of one or more units. If the recipient party is a consumer, the externality is represented as an additional variable in his utility function

$$u_B = u_B(q_1, \ldots, q_n, x_A)$$

where the q's are activities under B's control (usually goods B purchases) and x_A is the activity under A's control.

I shall not consider externalities where any of the parties are consumers so as to avoid the utility measurement problem when I come to dealing with taxes and subsidies. Much of the literature makes this "cop-out," particularly that part of the literature involving explicit tax/subsidy calculating schemes. This courageous approach can perhaps be justified on the grounds that we should examine the merit of the tax/subsidy approach in the simpler case of externalities among firms (where dollar measurement poses no difficulties) before putting a great deal of effort into more difficult applications. This is particularly appropriate in light of the recent literature which questions the validity of the Pigovian approach in general.

Thus I shall consider only externalities among producers. The externality can be represented as an additional variable in the recipient's cost function

$$k_B = k_B(q_1, \ldots, q_L, x_A)$$

where the q's are outputs under B's control. Although the environmental externalities currently in vogue generally affect consumers directly, the category of externalities among producers is not an empty box. Environmental externalities clearly affect producers. (The surfaces of New York's offices and commercial buildings deteriorate from air pollution; a plant upstream raises the temperature of the water supply for cooling of plants downstream.) Perhaps most importantly, inventions and pure research constitute externalities for producers. Since a great deal of our economic growth comes from this source, its optimization is important.

6

Often A's activity affects several firms[4] and sometimes the externalities are mutual (that is, A's activity affects B and B's activity affects A). Thus we may find a group of firms which may not be broken down into subgroups between which no externality relation exists. We say this group is connected by an interdependent set of production externalities.

There are two other facts we should note about the definition. The first is that it excludes from our consideration pecuniary externalities. These externalities (such as a decreasing long-run supply curve for a competitive industry—external economies of industry scale) do not result in misallocation of resources, so we need not give them the same treatment as technological externalities.[5] The second fact is hidden a little better. The essential character of an externality, which arises from this definition, is that its "output" level is positive in market equilibrium. When you reflect on it, this seems strange. An ordinary good will not be produced if its market price is zero (which is what we mean when we say A is not compensated). We shall make use of that characteristic in developing a general externality production function.

SETTING OF THE EXTERNALITY PROBLEM. We assume an economy of N consumers and R firms acting as perfect competitors in product and factor markets, each trying to maximize its utility or profit respectively.[6] Assume for generality that all R firms (they are not necessarily all in the same industry) are affected by externalities.[7]

The reason for insisting on perfect competition everywhere is to avoid problems arising from the theorem of "second best" welfare optima. The

[4] The fact that several firms are affected often but not always means that the externality has the character of a public good. This relation will be explored in chapter 2.

[5] Thus technological externalities represent only a special case of interdependence among decision units. Note also that consumers are affected only indirectly (through output levels and prices of final products) by externalities among producers. Thus technological externalities among producers are only pecuniary externalities for consumers.

[6] Any of the firms may be earning Ricardian rent at equilibrium. Wellisz (1964) has shown that externalities would offer no allocative problem if there were no rent on resources supplied by the owners of the firm. Without rent, the introduction of external diseconomies would just mean that resources would switch to other uses in long-run equilibrium and this would be socially desirable, since there is always a cost to reducing the externality.

[7] We could assume that a subset of the firms is connected by an interdependent set of externalities, but it is simpler to find a Pareto optimum for all at once and avoid reallocating resources among subsets.

7

"second best" theorem tells us that if there are many departures from the conditions for a Pareto optimum, correcting some of them cannot be proved to be an improvement.[8] Thus, for example, Wellisz (1964) and Buchanan (1969) have shown that an attempt to correct an external diseconomy, by bargains or by taxes/subsidies, may lead to *less* socially desirable output levels if the producer of the external diseconomy is a monopolist. Although some work is going on with the object of limiting the scope of the "second best" theorem,[9] it is far safer for the present to assume that there are no departures from the Pareto optimality conditions except the presence of externalities.

The Pigovian approach to externalities is to impose taxes or subsidies on the firms experiencing externalities so as to restore them to a Pareto optimum at equilibrium.[10] The approach assumes that if we restore Pareto optimality in the production sector and the conditions for Pareto optimality are already met in the consumption sector (perfect competition assures this), then resource allocation is Pareto optimal in the entire system.[11]

1.3. Survey of the externality literature

This section surveys the literature on the two subjects which take up the most space in this book and are probably the most important. One is the issue of what formal model of externalities to use. The second part of this section therefore serves as an introduction to chapter 2 by setting forth what I call the traditional model of externalities and ferreting out the

[8] Lancaster and Lipsey (1956–57).

[9] See, for example, Davis and Whinston (1965), (1967), McManus (1967), McFadden (1969).

[10] A Pareto optimum is defined here as a situation where no consumer's utility can be increased without reducing some other consumer's utility, and no saleable output can be increased without reducing some other saleable output or increasing some costly input.

[11] It would be somewhat more general if we formulated a single model for both consumption and production sectors. Following Lange (1942), the quantities of factors of production supplied by individuals would appear in their utility functions as well as in the firms' production functions, and their factor incomes (including net rent) would constrain their purchases. We would then set taxes/subsidies on externalities to enforce the simultaneously determined Pareto optimum. The approach we use for finding taxes/subsidies to enforce optimality in the production sector could be used as well to enforce an overall optimum, since it is designed to enforce any set of output levels which is Pareto optimal.

properties which I believe make it too narrow a representation. Chapter 2 then develops, and the rest of the book uses, the replacement model, based on a generalized joint product approach. The other subject covered in this section is the rather extensive body of literature proposing and opposing the "Pigovian" solution of taxes and subsidies. Since I shall devote a great deal of space to developing a tax/subsidy scheme which avoids some of the problems noted by the critics of previous schemes, it is only fair to begin by surveying the literature of criticism.

THE PIGOVIAN TRADITION AND ITS DISMANTLING. Ever since Marshall, externalities have been a principal flaw in the static theory of pure competition. Proofs that pure competition results in an optimal allocation of resources invariably exclude the case where one firm confers on another a benefit or a cost outside the market mechanism. Pigou (1932 and earlier editions) made the first attempt to resolve the externality problem. Pigou's welfare criterion is that the national dividend is maximized when values of marginal social net products (computed without regard to whom they accrue) are equal in all uses. Under perfect competition, values of marginal private net products are equal in all uses, so his welfare criterion is met if marginal social and private net products are the same. Pigou states two general cases where, under competition, marginal social and private net products may diverge. In the first case there are uncompensated services or disservices to the general public arising from the production of a good or service. In the second, a competitive industry has an increasing or decreasing long-run supply price as industry output increases.[12] In both of these cases, Pigou concluded that if marginal social net product exceeds marginal private net product, the output attained under competition will be less than the ideal output, and the opposite will hold if marginal social net product is less than marginal private net product.

Pigou proposed the device of taxes and bounties to guide the firms producing externalities, by a modified invisible hand, to the ideal output which maximizes national dividend. By his reasoning, if marginal social exceeds marginal private net product there is an optimum *bounty* which makes them equal and causes the firms, in maximizing individual profit, to produce the ideal output. If marginal social net product is less than

[12] The present work is concerned solely with the first case, that of technological externalities, as noted in section 1.2.

marginal private net product, there is an optimum *tax* which makes them equal. Stated in a more modern way: "The Pigovian problem is to impose upon each firm a tax which internalizes the external effects so that each firm will choose the socially optimal output by considering its price and its own marginal costs (including the tax) without taking into account any other factors."[13] Although Pigou was unable to specify the means by which they would be computed, he was convinced that a *determinate* scheme of optimal taxes and bounties exists for every case. He conceded that large administrative costs might be incurred in real life and that a tax or bounty computed blindly might be so large as to do more harm than good.

When the "new welfare economics" came along, with Pareto optimality as the strongest welfare criterion that can be deduced "scientifically," it was soon shown that externalities can cause an equilibrium in an otherwise perfectly competitive system to violate the conditions for Pareto optimality. Rigorous proof of this is to be found in such standard price theory texts as Henderson and Quandt (1958).

Since Pigou, although much definition and classification of externalities have been done, there were, until recent years, few notable attempts to prove or disprove Pigou's theory that taxes and subsidies can give firms experiencing externalities incentive to produce the socially optimal outputs. Meade (1952) showed how to derive ad valorem taxes and subsidies for the special case of a production function homogenous of degree one. It must be emphasized that this is a very special case, because there is considerable and growing evidence that the individual plant or firm cost curve is U-shaped or declining in the relevant region.[14] (It is true, of course, that firms are likely, *ceteris paribus*, to be operating in the constant returns portion of their cost curves, if we assume pure competition and no Ricardian rent, but this does not prove that the entire cost curve shows constant returns at every point.) The Pigovian theory, fortified by specific tax/subsidy schemes, has managed to creep into such standard textbooks as Henderson and Quandt's *Microeconomic Theory* (1958) without significant challenge.

The work of Coase (1960) provides the first powerful attack on the Pigovian approach or, rather, its blind application. The most important feature of Coase's attack is his emphasis on the total social product of

[13] Wellisz (1964), pp. 359–360.
[14] See Haldi and Whitcomb (1967).

10

alternative arrangements of resources. His best example of the need to examine alternative social arrangements is that of a factory which causes smoke damage estimated at $100 per annum to surrounding firms. If the factory is taxed $100 so long as it emits smoke, it will install a smoke-preventing device costing, say, $90 per year.

Yet the position achieved by the Pigovian tax is not optimal. Suppose that those who suffer the damage could avoid it by moving to other locations or by taking various precautions which would cost them, or be equivalent to a loss in income of, $40 per annum. Then there would be a gain in the value of production of $50 if the factory continued to emit its smoke and those now in the district moved elsewhere or made other adjustments to avoid the damage.[15,16]

Thus Coase brings to externalities the opportunity cost emphasis of price theory. In addition to considering the social product of the firms as the amount of the externality varies, we must also consider the social product if some of the firms move into another line of business.

Although skeptical of the possibility of using taxes to enforce his broader conception of a socially optimal arrangement of resources, Coase does not reject it out of hand. It is clear that he considers a revamped Pigovian approach as an alternative to administrative enforcement of socially optimal output levels and to decentralized solutions. Coase's contributions to this approach will be discussed farther along in this section; the significance of his work to the approach used in this paper will be discussed at the end of section 3.2. I believe that it is possible theoretically to determine, from the information used in computing taxes and subsidies, whether a firm should give up its present line of business or move to another location, and then use the tax or subsidy to effect the correct solution. If resources are really valued at opportunity cost in a firm's cost functions, this is easy to do; if not, it is difficult and costly, but not impossible. One must count this part of Coase's work as a necessary and helpful modification of the Pigovian approach.

[15] Coase (1960), p. 41. Note that Coase's welfare criterion for production externalities among competitive firms is that the combined profit of the firms affected by the externalities be at a maximum. This criterion is accepted by all modern writers.

[16] But note that the free market will enforce this decision without state intervention. The pool of such situations will be very small because of the action of the market. Therefore state intervention will be called on mainly in cases where it can improve the situation.

There is more to his attack on the Pigovian tradition. Coase cites the lack of detail and the qualifications made by Pigou himself and notes with some surprise the near unanimity of modern economists in the belief that a tax based on damages caused or a subsidy based on benefits conferred will impel firms to produce socially optimal outputs. Then Coase makes a very important distinction: "As it is not proposed that the proceeds of the tax be paid to those suffering the damage, this solution [a tax equal to the damage done] is not the same as that which would force a business to pay compensation to those damaged by its actions, although economists generally do not seem to have noticed this and tend to treat the two solutions as being identical."[17] Coase did not pursue this distinction. Buchanan and Stubblebine (1962) and Turvey (1963) carried the distinction one step farther, showing that if the tax is *not* paid to the injured firm and if the firms are able to negotiate, a nonoptimal solution will result. This implies a modification of the Pigovian scheme: "There is a necessity for any impost levied on A to be paid to B when A and B are able to negotiate."[18]

Since about the time Coase wrote, another Pigovian approach has become popular. Under this approach, instead of being based on damage or benefit, a tax or subsidy is computed whose purpose is to make each firm produce socially optimal levels of outputs under its control. The resulting tax or subsidy is a constant multiplied by the externality level. Writers favoring or citing[19] this approach also do not propose that the tax or subsidy be paid to the firm affected by the externality. One would expect that Buchanan and Stubblebine's and Turvey's conclusion would apply to this scheme as well. In section 3.4, I shall class as "standard" Pigovian approaches both the tax based on damages and the tax whose purpose is to encourage socially optimal outputs rather than to make compensation. That section will demonstrate that neither "standard" approach will work if the tax or subsidy is not paid to the recipient of the externality.

So far, the attack on the Pigovian tradition has only succeeded in forcing a modification of tax/subsidy schemes. The question the attackers now turn themselves to is whether the modified schemes are workable. One

[17] Coase (1960), p. 41.

[18] Turvey (1963), p. 311.

[19] Henderson and Quandt (1958), Davis and Whinston (1962) and (1967), and MacManus (1967).

must distinguish two lines of attack. The first is the contention that it is difficult and/or very costly to get correct information on the profit functions of firms. It becomes a matter of judgment (and the judgment often seems to reflect political philosophy) as to whether the results are worth the difficulties and cost. Although theoretical light can be cast on whether firms have incentive to give correct information, welfare economics has nothing to say once we admit of some degree of imperfection in information.

The other line of attack is more immediate and can be handled with theoretical analysis. It is an assertion that even with perfect, costless information available to the "center," tax/subsidy schemes cannot always enforce Pareto optimal output levels.

Davis and Whinston (1962) claimed that there is a theoretically possible class of externalities, mutual nonseparable externalities—that is, where profit of firm 1 is a nonseparable function of that firm's output and an output controlled by firm 2, $P_1(q_1, q_2)$ cannot be written as $P_{11}(q_1) + P_{12}(q_2)$ and vice versa for firm 2; see section 4.5—where no tax/subsidy scheme can give the firms incentive to produce socially optimal outputs. Their argument was based on the uncertainty inherent when one firm's decision rule includes as a variable the other firm's output. "There seems to be *no a priori method* for determining the outputs (strategies) selected. Non-separable externalities raise the possibility of the non-existence of equilibrium."[20] The imposition of Pigovian taxes does not improve the chances for reaching equilibrium, the authors claim.

However, in the non-separable externality case, even assuming that the governmental policy-maker knows the relevant cost functions and desires to maximize welfare, there seems to be no dominant solution to aim at . . . . In fact, for the policy-maker to be able to determine the strategy which individual firms might be playing, it would seem necessary, in the absence of a priori methods, to obtain information concerning the psychologies of the managers, their taste for risk, and so on . . . the classical tax-subsidy solution . . .breaks down for this non-separable type of externality.[21]

Davis and Whinston used their analysis on a scheme where a constant tax per unit of externality is (implied to be) paid to the government instead of to the externality recipient.[22] The analysis of Buchanan and

[20] Davis and Whinston (1962), p. 255.
[21] *Ibid.*, p. 256.
[22] See *ibid.*, p. 251.

13

Stubblebine (1962) and Turvey (1963) is sufficient to destroy these schemes, as we have seen. However, the Davis-Whinston analysis would seem to apply to cases where the tax (whether based on damages or per unit of externality) is paid to the party affected. Turvey seems to think so,[23] and the deep quiet on the externality front that has prevailed since then would seem to imply that others think so too. We shall show in section 3.4 that this conclusion is justified for taxes based on damages.

Wellisz (1964) showed that a tax/subsidy scheme can be derived which eliminates any uncertainty in a firm's decision rule arising from nonseparability and gives the firm incentive to produce socially optimal externality levels. In this scheme, a nonproportional charge can be found which, when added to the firm's profit function, gives the firm a revised profit function whose maximum does not depend on the other firm's output. Professor Wellisz's scheme is in fact a quite general proof that there does exist a determinate tax/subsidy scheme having the properties sought by Pigou. Davis and Whinston (1966) attacked Wellisz's scheme on the ground that it necessitated solving differential equations for which no truly general solution methods exist. If granted, their criticism still does not detract from Wellisz's theoretical confirmation of Pigou's intuition although it does raise doubts as to the number of cases in which the charge can be found.

Here the prosecution rests, and the defense hasn't produced any new witnesses lately. Testimony will be introduced in chapter 4 setting forth a per-unit tax/subsidy scheme (a constant, assigned "shadow price") which gets around the nonseparability problem and can be found for any firms with "well-behaved" cost functions.[24]

An entirely different school of thought about achieving optimal allocation under externalities, which has arisen in recent years, can be classed under the general heading of decentralized approaches to the externality problem. One wing of this school is the "private bargaining solution" approach, which seems to have been put forward authoritatively first by Coase (1960) and represented since then by Buchanan and Stubblebine (1962), Turvey (1963), and Buchanan (1966). This approach represents an attack on the Pigovian tradition of the most powerful sort: in its boldest form it says taxes and subsidies *are not needed*. This approach holds that,

[23] Turvey (1963), pp. 311–312.
[24] And for many without. See Appendixes C and D.

since the socially optimal outputs are those which maximize combined profit of the firms affected by externalities, the firms themselves have incentive to *agree* to produce the optimal outputs and then distribute the profit such that each firm's profit is greater than or equal to the profit it could earn by maximizing individually without bargaining. Thus, by this reasoning, state intervention is unnecessary to achieve a social optimum except to enforce bargains freely agreed to.

Coase therefore concluded that bargaining makes irrelevant any legal requirement that a party be liable for its damages, the same optimal allocation of resources resulting whether or not the damage creator is liable for his damages.[25] This led Turvey (1963) to state that "whether or not we should advocate the imposition of a liability on A for damages caused is a matter of fairness, not of resource allocation."[26] However, Dolbear (1967) showed, for consumption externalities, that the existence of legal responsibility does affect the level of externality output achieved in private bargaining among consumers. This would modify the Coase-Turvey conclusion to state that Pareto efficient outputs will be produced whether or not the damage-creator is liable for his damages, but for consumption externalities, the outputs will not necessarily be the same. We will reach a point on the efficiency frontier, but not necessarily the same point.

The proponents of the private bargain solution generally make parenthetical qualifications on their strong conclusion. For example, Coase states that "the ultimate result (which maximizes the value of production) is independent of the legal position if the pricing system is assumed to work without cost."[27] It is not clear whether this phrase (which he uses twice) is intended to mean "if bargains can be reached," or "if the cost of time, etc., spent on bargains (which can certainly be reached) is less than the worth of the bargain." There is some evidence in favor of the latter interpretation.[28] Buchanan and Stubblebine (1962), in a passing reference to private bargains (for which they use the phrase "trade"), do not even qualify their conclusion parenthetically: "A can surely work out some means of compensating B in exchange for B's agreement to reduce the

---

[25] Coase (1960), pp. 427–429.
[26] Turvey (1963), p. 311.
[27] Coase (1960), p. 428.
[28] See *ibid.*, p. 430.

15

scope of the activity. . . ."[29] The implication is very strong that bargains can always be treated as an alternative to Pigovian methods: "If a tax/ subsidy method, rather than 'trade' is to be introduced . . . . "[30]

Turvey (1963) was the first bargaining proponent to make a reasonably precise qualification: "We now turn to the case where A and B cannot negotiate, which in most cases will result from A and/or B being too large a group for the members to get together . . . there is thus a case for collective action to achieve optimum allocation."[31] Once such qualifications as this are made, black-and-white arguments on the validity of the bargaining solution can no longer be made. One can question the relative emphasis, however. The articles I have cited all seem to leave the impression that bargains are likely enough to occur (and the difficulties with the Pigovian approach are great enough) so that alternatives to private bargains are not attractive. My own view is that optimal bargains are so unlikely to occur that we must study the alternatives. We may yet find the alternatives unworkable, of course.

Game theoretic arguments are used by Wellisz (1964) to show that the bargaining solution breaks down when large groups are involved in the bargaining. The essence of his position is that each firm sees itself as a "free rider" on a bargain negotiated and paid for by the other firms affected. If enough firms see themselves this way, a bargain will not come about. This consideration apparently led Buchanan (1966) to back off somewhat from his previous position. "The analysis, therefore, allows us to 'explain' the pressures toward equilibrium, through ordinary trading processes if the interacting groups are critically small, or through the working of the political process if the interacting group becomes critically large . . . ."[32] It is still implied that, with small groups, optimal bargains are likely, although some softening of even this position is seen in the quote above ("pressures toward equilibrium," not "how equilibrium will be reached") and in the following: "Trade will tend to take place until the

[29] Buchanan and Stubblebine (1962), p. 380.

[30] *Ibid.*, p. 383.

[31] Turvey (1963), p. 312.

[32] Buchanan (1966), pp. 414–415. The point Buchanan makes about pressure toward equilibrium through the working of the political process is most interesting, but it cannot be pursued here. A number of articles in this area have appeared in recent years in the journal *Papers on Non-Market Decision Making* of the Thomas Jefferson Center of the University of Virginia.

difficulty of calculating Pigovian taxes/subsidies, said:

How much B suffers will in many cases depend not only upon the *scale* of A's diseconomy-creating activity, but also upon the precise *nature* of A's activity and upon B's *reaction* to it. If A emits smoke, for example, B's loss will depend not only upon the quantity emitted but also upon the height of A's chimney and upon the cost to B of installing air-conditioning, indoor clothes-dryers or other means of reducing the effect of the smoke. Thus to ascertain the optimum resource allocation will frequently require an investigation of the nature and costs both of alternative devices open to A and of the devices by which B can reduce the impact of each activity.[36]

Coase (1960) makes essentially the same point in several examples. However, in the literature the formal analysis continues to be conducted in terms of the traditional model. Only one author, Buchanan (1966), has attempted to develop a generalization of the formal model. We shall discuss his important contribution toward the end of section 2.1, where it can be assessed better.

The production function which gives rise to the cost function $k_i(q)$ is identical in form to the one Marshall used in his beef and hides example of joint products. Shoup (1965) gives the name "strict" joint production to such joint products. It is worthwhile to look closely at this kind of production function as applied to externalities. Take firm j which produces one of the externalities affecting firm i in model (1.3.1) above. My favorite example is New York's Consolidated Edison. It produces electricity (q_j) and smoke (x_j), an externality. Firm i, the recipient, might be an outdoor laundry, or, more realistically, a firm which is concerned about the appearance of its building. Firm j's production function consists of two equations:

(a) $\quad q_j = f(v_1, \ldots, v_n, \ldots, v_N)$

(b) $\quad x_j = g(q_j)$ \hfill (1.3.2)

(The v_n are a set of inputs.)

The transformation curve arising from this production set is typical of strict joint products. If we hold constant all inputs, v_n, then q_j, the remaining argument in equation (a), is fixed at some particular value. Then x_j in equation (b) is also fixed. This corresponds to point A in Figure 1. The

---

[36] Turvey (1963), p. 309.

transformation curve is a point in $q_j - x_j$ space. If we could "waste" either of the outputs, the transformation curve would be BAC, but that is not possible here. The only valuable joint product is q_j, so there is no point in wasting some of it (as there might be with two or more valuable joint products—e.g., beef and hides). The externality is of course "wasted" already so far as firm j is concerned. In the sense that we use "waste" here, however, the externality cannot be wasted—the recipient firm gets the amount x_j regardless.

The curve labeled "g" in Figure 1 is the locus of points like "A" for all possible combinations of constant input levels. Note that if, instead of

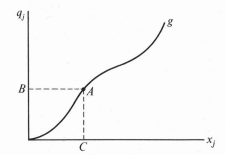

FIGURE 1

Transformation curve with externality a strict joint product

equation (1.3.2) (b), we have $x_j = aq_j$ where a is a constant, then we have the special case of fixed output proportions where g is a straight line. The traditional model of externalities does not necessarily require a production model this restrictive.

It is easy to see how the traditional externalities model implies the production function (1.3.2). The recipient firm's cost of producing q_i is affected by the level of x_j, so we might have x_j as a variable in the cost function, k_i. However, since $x_j = g(q_j)$, we can rewrite k_i with q_j as a function. With any production function where g contains some variable other than q_j, we will not be able to rewrite k_i in this manner.[37]

---

[37] The chances are that model (1.3.2) doesn't even fit the beef and hides example well, although that is more the "fault" of modern technology than of Marshall. If we take a fairly long-term view, it is not hard to imagine varying the inputs so as to alter the level of beef production for a given hide production (measured in square feet). This can be done by varying the food composition or the breeding stock so as to produce larger or smaller cattle. The volume (beef) will increase at a different rate than the surface area (hides). The situation is still appropriately described by the term "joint production" but the model (2.1.2), introduced in the next chapter, fits it better.

20

Before we go on, there is one other fact worth noting about (1.3.2). Equation (b) makes it impossible for firm j to alter the externality level by using extra inputs, while holding q_j constant.

Now back to Con Ed. The traditional model of externalities would have us alter the level of electricity output in order to produce the "optimal" amount of smoke. In fact, what Con Ed does when it is required to reduce its smoke output is to build higher smokestacks, use a different grade of fuel, or switch to nuclear power. A useful economic model should not altogether ignore these alternatives.

What will be called in this paper a "generalized joint production" model offers a unified and general approach to externalities among firms. The next chapter will be devoted to developing that model and showing how it offers greater realism. Succeeding chapters will develop results on externality taxes and subsidies for the generalized joint production model. These results could have been developed for the traditional model, but it seemed desirable to make them apply to a larger class of situations.

TWO

A MODEL OF GENERALIZED JOINT PRODUCTION

The purpose of this chapter is to develop production and cost functions general enough to encompass several varieties of externalities and to eliminate the restrictions noted in the last chapter. Section 2.1 will develop (in several steps) a generalized version of the joint product production function which suits our requirements and discuss the background of this approach in the literature. We will extend the notation of the production function model to the case where there are many firms affected by an interdependent set of externalities, having some characteristics of public goods. The following section will rigorously derive a cost function in which saleable outputs and externalities are variables.

2.1. *The production function model*

The kind of model needed to represent the production of externalities realistically can be seen most easily by drawing the kind of cost curves needed. In Figure 2, the total cost of producing a fixed level of the saleable output q_j is represented as a function of the externality level, x_j. The curve shown conveys the central idea of an externality; namely, that, without being paid for it, firm j produces some positive finite amount of the externality. Call this level $\hat{x}_j$ in Figure 2. A rational firm will produce this level only if it is cheaper than producing some other amount or none at all of the externality. If we also insist that it is *possible* to produce other levels of the externality while holding q_j constant, we have the total cost curve shown.[1] The locus of all minimum-cost points as we change $\bar{q}_j$ is the curve "k_j min." It also represents the only points allowed by the traditional model of externalities. (In saying this, we give the traditional model the benefit of the doubt. We *assume* the function $x_j = g(q_j)$ allows firm j to produce cost-minimizing x_j rather than some less efficient but equally restrictive locus giving a one-to-one relationship between x_j and q_j.)

The traditional model is therefore not a bad representation of a world in which nothing (neither private bargains nor taxes/subsidies) can be done about externalities. It is only when we come to consider remedies that it is

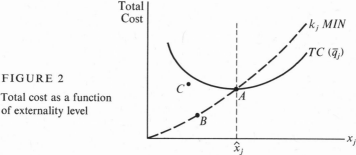

FIGURE 2

Total cost as a function of externality level

too restrictive a model. Assume that x_j is an external diseconomy, smoke and that its level of production, $\hat{x}_j$, is "too high" according to Pareto efficiency criteria. An efficient solution, *if the world really looked like the traditional model*, might involve moving along "k_j min," to point B where a lot less electricity is produced as the price for getting less smoke. The more realistic model we are searching for might allow us to move to point C where we have given up very little electricity but have incurred a higher cost per unit. Since the new model does not rule out points like B, then if it is constructed so we can correctly evaluate the relative desirability of alternatives it must be true that C is better than B.[2]

Let us now develop the production function underlying the cost curve in Figure 2. We shall return to cost functions in section 2 of this chapter.

The trouble with the production function (1.3.2) implied by the traditional model of externalities is that once you have set the saleable output,

[1] This curve implies an assumption of convexity which permits no other local minima than the global minimum at x_j. This will be justified in section 2.2.

[2] We haven't yet shown precise criteria for selecting optimal points; this we will do in chapter 3.

you have automatically fixed the externality level no matter what you do to the inputs. It's a problem of *too few* degrees of freedom. So it might seem that if we'd treat both the externality and the saleable output as variables in a single-equation production function, we'd have the right amount of flexibility.

$$q_j = f(x_j, v_1, \ldots, v_N)$$

or

$$F(q_j, x_j, v_1, \ldots, v_N) = 0 \tag{2.1.1}$$

This is an extension of the multi-product model used by Carlson (1939) and Hicks (1946) and now incorporated in most intermediate texts, e.g., Henderson and Quandt (1958).[3] The recipient firm would have a similar function, but with x_j appearing as a variable instead of q_j. That is, the firm receiving an externality treats it as an input with a zero price (unless some institutional arrangement creates a price). It is obvious that if we hold constant the level of q_j, we can alter the level of x_j by changing the amounts of some of the inputs. Thus the effect on the recipient firm is not tied rigidly to the level of q_j.

The trouble with *this* production function is that it gives us *too many* degrees of freedom. If we assume a given amount of all inputs, F becomes $F(q_j, x_j, \bar{v}_1, \ldots, \bar{v}_N) = 0$ and we can now call it a transformation function. Because it is one equation in two variables, we can vary the outputs at will, subject only to the technical limits given by F. Does this fit what we know about the way externalities are produced? Looking again at Con Ed, we see that it does not. If we have given amounts of all inputs, one of which is,

---

[3] Other kinds of multi-product production functions have been suggested. Danø (1966) recognizes the utility of (2.1.1) in cases where several outputs are produced in a single production process but shows that another model applies when each output has a separate process. A two-output, two-input version of that model is

$$q_1 = f_1(v_{11}, v_{12}); \qquad q_2 = f_2(v_{21}, v_{22})$$

$$v_1 = v_{11} + v_{21}; \qquad v_2 = v_{12} + v_{22}$$

Here the input v_1 can be separately allocated to process 1 or to process 2 or divided among them. We cannot really say for which output v_1 is used in model (2.1.1). In both models we can hold constant total quantities of each input available to the firm and alter output quantities along a transformation curve.

Because this is not primarily a work on production theory, we shall ignore all the other ways in which ordinary (saleable) outputs may be produced and assume that model (2.1.1) is a good enough representation, concentrating attention on externalities.

say, fuel oil type X, model (2.1.1) would imply that we can produce more electricity by changing the amount of smoke we produce. Of course we can't do this. The smoke is caused by the amount of fuel oil type X we burn, given the plant and other inputs. While we *can* vary the externality by changing the type of fuel oil, or perhaps the amount of other fixed or variable inputs, we cannot do so while all these things are held constant. The transformation curve between electricity and smoke is really a point for Con Ed; with fixed amounts of inputs it cannot vary the amounts of electricity and smoke.

The production function for an externality producer like Con Ed will look like this:[4]

(a) $F_1(q_j, v_1, v_2) = 0$

(b) $F_2(x_j, v_2, v_3) = 0$ (2.1.2)

If we hold inputs v_1, v_2, and v_3 constant, F_1 and F_2 both become equations in a single variable, determining unique values for q_j and x_j. Thus the transformation curve is a point. x_j is not represented as a function of q_j though, so we avoid the narrowness of the "strict" joint product model. Model (2.1.2) is a formalization of what Shoup (1965) called (in another context) a "broad" joint product model. One might also call it a "by-product" model.

Perhaps the most important thing about model (2.1.2) is its treatment of the input v_2. It appears in both of the equations, so we may call it a *joint* input. It is what makes joint products joint rather than separate in this formulation and it is central to the explanation of why we have externalities at all. To see why, consider one of the ordinary inputs, say v_3. Depending on the nature of the input, its total product curve with x_j as the product (other variables held constant) would look like panel (a) or (b) of Figure 3. In panel (a), v_3 fits the role we normally expect of an input. The more of it we use, the more x_j we get. This isn't of much relevance to an external diseconomy because nobody wants more of it, but it does apply where society has somehow induced a firm to expand its production of an external economy. But note that if the firm is left alone, it will use none of the input

---

[4] Essentially similar production functions are used by Henderson (1953), pp. 157 ff.; Frisch (1965), pp. 270 ff.; and Danø (1966), p. 188, for joint production in the absence of externalities.

25

to produce an externality which commands no price. We have no explanation yet of how an externality comes into being through a firm's private action. Panel (b) shows an input which can be used to reduce the amount produced of an external diseconomy. Again, a profit-maximizing firm will use none of the input to reduce its externality. And this doesn't explain how the externality got produced in the first place. Positive levels of an externality will only be produced (in the absence of outside pressure)

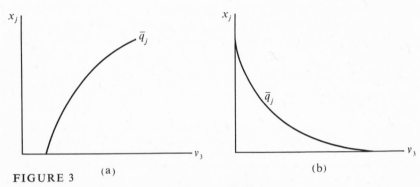

FIGURE 3   (a)   (b)

Externality total product curves for an ordinary input

when some input used in producing a saleable output produces the externality as a by-product. By treating the input v_2 as a variable in both the equation involving q_j and the equation involving x_j, our notation is made to convey that fact. Neither v_1 nor v_3 appears in both equations so neither produces one output as a by-product of producing the other. In a sense this is a more fundamental argument for using model (2.1.2) than the transformation function argument. Even in the case where we could imagine a transformation relation between the externality and the saleable output, we would still need a joint input to explain the existence of the externality. A production function like (2.1.2) implies that if we use any v_2 in producing the saleable output, then some of the externality will be produced, thanks to equation (b).[5] The single-equation model (2.1.1) implies just the opposite. x_j is an independent variable (or it wouldn't appear), so it can be zero with positive v_2 and positive with zero v_2.

[5] The x_1 total product curve for the joint input v_2 will be a point. v_2 appears in F_1, so if its level changes then q_j must change and that is not allowed by the usual *ceteris paribus* definition of a total product curve.

26

Production functions like model (2.1.2) would seem to cover a broad range of classes of externality. Most kinds of environmental pollution are produced in such a way that we can vary the ratio of pollutant to saleable output, but only by changing the amounts or types of inputs. These production functions are obviously relevant when we are considering the effect of environmental externalities on individuals' utility functions as well as producers' profit functions. Another important class of externality is inventions which are by-products of a company's research on lowering its production cost or improving its product. In spite of patent laws (really, often because of them), inventions are made which help another firm develop a new product or lower its cost of production.[6] The "quantity" of inventions is not fixed for each level of saleable output. But where one resource, like scientific manpower, is used only for making inventions useful in producing the saleable output, a fixed quantity of it and other resources will result in a certain number of "company" inventions and therefore in a fixed number of "by-product inventions," which are the externality.

It may be that the scientific manpower of a firm could work directly on inventions useful to others rather than going the indirect route which results in "by-product inventions." In this case, we could vary the externality level while holding all inputs fixed, and saleable output would presumably vary in some inverse relation. This can be treated as an extension of model (2.1.2).

$$F_1(q_j, v_1, v_2, v_{13}) = 0$$
$$F_2(x_j, v_2, v_{23}) = 0$$
$$v_3 = v_{13} + v_{23} \tag{2.1.3}$$

By the basic definition of an externality, we must assume that the externality will appear even if the firm exhibits no altruism, so we must retain the joint input v_2. Say it is a kind of scientific manpower not capable of going the direct route. A closely related input is v_3, scientific personnel who can work on inventions useful to the firm *or* on inventions useful to others.

---

[6] Patent laws are a device to help "internalize" an externality, i.e., to give a firm the incentive to produce the socially optimal "quantity" of inventions. Like other real-world devices for dealing with externalities, such as zoning laws, they are imperfect. A good case can be made for studying invention externalities to try to improve or supplement the incentive devices we now have.

The firm can allocate v_3 as its "social conscience" or whatever directs. We shall include inputs like this in our standard model from now on, recognizing that they may not always appear in all situations. In fact, we can use this to replace the notation we have used for v_1, as that can get unwieldy when we generalize to R firms and M externalities. We can write $v_1 = v_{11} + v_{21}$, but if this input cannot be used in F_2, then v_{21} will never appear. In general, both the "strict" joint product formulation and the single-equation model can be profitably thought of as special cases of model (2.1.3). Since this model and its special cases also cover most kinds of joint and multiple production of ordinary goods, it seems fair to call it a generalized joint production model.

AN R-FIRM PRODUCTION FUNCTION MODEL. This subsection introduces the model which will be used throughout the rest of the monograph. It is an extension of the production function notation developed above to an economy of many firms, each using several inputs and producing several outputs. The only new analysis is the explicit treatment of externalities as public goods and the incorporation of this into the notation.

The production function is

$$F_{i1}(q_i, X_{i1}, v_{i1}^n, v_i^p) = 0 \qquad (i = 1, \ldots, R$$

$$F_{ik}(x_{i0m}, v_{ik}^n, v_i^p) = 0 \qquad m = 1, \ldots, M$$

$$v_{in} = \sum_{k=1}^{K} v_{ikn} \qquad k = m + 1 = 2, \ldots, K \qquad (2.1.4)$$

$$n = 1, \ldots, N)^7$$

where

$q_i = (q_{i1}, \ldots, q_{iL})$; a vector of saleable outputs of firm i, where q_{i1} is the output by i of product 1.

$X_{i1} = (x_{j0m})_{j,m}$ $(j = 1, \ldots, R, \neq i; m = 1, \ldots, M)$, a $(R-1)$ by M matrix of externalities received by firm i. Externalities produced by i do not appear in F_{i1}. x_{j0m} is the amount of externality type m produced by j and received by all other firms, including i.

$x_{i0m} = $ an externality produced by firm i and received by all other firms.

[7] We note again that input n may appear in only one or in more than one of the equations of i's production set. Unlike input p, its appearance in two or more equations is an act of conscious allocation on the firm's part.

$v_{ik}^n = (v_{ik1}, \ldots, v_{ikN})$; a vector of ordinary inputs to equation k of firm i's production set.

$v_i^p = (v_{i1}, \ldots, v_{iP})$; a vector of joint inputs appearing in all equations of firm i's production set.

The externality notation needs some further explanation since it will be used throughout the rest of the paper. Externalities usually have the character of public goods because "use" of an externality by one firm does not reduce the amount available for any other firm. We assume here that the amount produced by firm i equals the amount received by firm $1, \ldots$, equals the amount received by firm R.[8] Most of the environmental externalities of current interest, such as pollution, are of the public good variety; and we shall conduct our analysis under this assumption.

The treatment of externalities as public (or collective) goods goes back at least as far as Bator (1958), and is implicit in Buchanan and Stubblebine (1962) and other articles. An explicit public goods notation, somewhat different from mine, is found in Mishan (1969).

One may wonder what distinguishes externalities from other public goods. It is that externalities are always produced as by-products of some other activity. Public goods of the Bowen-Lindahl-Samuelson variety are not necessarily by-products. They may be formulated as single products or as multiple products as in model (2.1.1); in special cases they may be efficiently produced as "narrow" or "broad" joint products.

Some externalities produced by one firm may affect several recipient firms, but nevertheless have some of the character of private goods. Meade's orchard and bees example is cited by Bator (1958) as such a case. "Apple blossoms are . . . an ordinary, private, exhaustible good; the more nectar for one bee, the less for another."[9] The distinguishing feature of

---

[8] For some kinds of externality (smoke is an example) we might assume the amount of the externality received by j is a function of the amount produced by i and that the function varies from firm to firm (depending in the case of smoke, for example, on the distance from the source). Thus we would get relations of the form $x_{ijm} = f_{ijm}(x_{iim})$, where the second subscript refers to the firm measuring the externality level. The public good character would still be preserved when we write the inverse functions: $x_{iim} = f_{i1m}^{-1}(x_{i1m}) = f_{i2m}^{-1}(x_{i2m}) = \cdots = f_{iRm}^{-1}(x_{iRm})$. I have chosen not to incorporate this assumption explicitly in the notation because it becomes too intricate. Instead I assume the recipient's production function reflects the effect of distance, for example, in the relationship it states between x_{i0m} and the other variables. The analytical conclusions are the same.

[9] Bator (1958), p. 364.

these "ownership externalities" (in Bator's classification scheme) is the impossibility of excluding any recipient from "enjoying" them (this applies to diseconomies as well as economies). Otherwise, they would be ordinary private goods, and market allocation would be efficient. "The difficulty is due exclusively to the difficulty of keeping accounts on the nectar-take of Capulet bees as against Montague bees."[10]

Unfortunately, we cannot formulate this type of externalities as private goods in the producer's F in any of the usual ways. For example, if we were to write $F_{ik}(x_{i1m}, \ldots, x_{iRm}, v_{ip}) = 0$ or $F_{ik}(\sum_{j=1}^{R \neq i} x_{ijm}, v_{ip}) = 0$, this would imply that we can change x_{i1m} by changing v_{ip} without changing x_{i2m}. This is not reasonable: the orchardist cannot always reduce the nectar going to Capulet's bees without reducing that going to Montague's. Because (as Bator noted) it is hard to find many cases of this type of externality, we do not explore the problems of formulating this type here.

There are two other points to be emphasized about the notation. An externality of type m must appear in the producer firm's $m + 1st$ production function (F_{ik}, $k = m + 1$) because of the "by-product" formulation which we must apply to any externality. Also some of the elements of X_{i1} and some of the x_{i0m} may not appear. A number of the M externality types may not be produced by firm i and others may not be received by it.

EARLIER WORK IN THIS AREA. Let us trace the developments in the literature that have led to this approach. The germ of this approach was seen as far back as Meade (1952). "So far throughout this note we have assumed that in all external economies and diseconomies ... it is the output of one industry that affects production in the other. But this is, of course, not necessarily the case. It may be the employment of one factor in one industry which confers an indirect benefit or the reverse upon producers in the other industry."[11] Meade's (first-degree homogeneous) production function embodying this concept is $x_1 = H_1(l_1, c_1, l_2)$ where x_1 is the saleable output of firm 1, l_1, and c_1 its factors of production, and l_2 a factor employed by another firm. In this construction it is possible to vary the level of the externality without varying x_2 (the saleable output of firm 2) by the same proportion. Meade did not pursue this characteristic of his model, however; and writers following him seem to have ignored it.

---

[10] *Ibid.*, p. 365.
[11] Meade (1952), p. 65.

An example suggested by Coase (1960), and cited in chapter 1, *implies* a production function like (2.1.4). If a factory producing $100 per year of smoke damage can install a smoke-preventing device costing $90 per year, it clearly can change the proportion between its saleable output and its externality.

An approach based on joint products was set forth explicitly first by Buchanan (1966). This important article treated externalities among consumers but at least parts of the analysis are relevant to the production

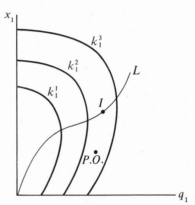

FIGURE 4

Isocost curves for an externality producer.
Source: Adapted from Buchanan (1966),
Figure 1, p. 411.

externality problem.[12] Buchanan proposed that we treat externalities as a special case of joint production wherein the externality x_1 is produced as a consequence of producing (or consuming) the valuable product q_1 and transferred (without choice or charge) to the other firm or person involved. Although he did not use the terminology, it is quite clear that he meant "broad" joint product, in the sense that it is possible to vary the proportion of externality to saleable output. This approach led Buchanan to develop a graphical analysis in which his isocost curves are the element most directly applicable to the problems we wish to consider here.

Let us examine a production externalities version of Buchanan's construction, Figure 4. Firm 1 produces a saleable output, q_1, having a competitive market price, and a joint product, x_1, which it gives away. (In fact, the affected firm cannot refuse it.) If we are able to vary the

[12] I shall recast his argument in terms of production externalities and in notation consistent with that used throughout this monograph.

31

proportions of q_1 and x_1, we can trace out locuses of constant-cost combinations of the two outputs. These are the isocost curves, labeled k_1^1, k_1^2, and k_1^3.[13] For each level of q_1, there is a level of x_1 (possibly 0, in which case we have no externality) at which q_1 can be produced at least cost. This level of x_1 and the corresponding q_1 is given by the locus of points, L, at which the isocost curves are vertical. Because x_1 commands no price, Firm 1 will choose only points along the locus L. At some point along L, Firm 1's profit will be at a maximum, say at point I. However, at some other point, generally *off* L, combined profit of the affected firms is maximized, say at $P.O.$[14]

Buchanan also presents a transformation function for an individual who produces joint, as well as ordinary, outputs. An example of the transformation function is

$$F^i = F^i(x_{y_a, y_b}, x_{y_c})$$

Here x_{y_a, y_b} represents joint supply, where x is a unit of production (a steer, for example) which embodies two consumption goods, y_a (beef) and y_b (hides).[15] x_{y_c} is an ordinary good.

This transformation function does not explicitly embody the flexibility of Buchanan's isocost curves. It simply states that we can produce, with given inputs, different quantity combinations of steers and the ordinary good. The proportion between consumption goods y_a and y_b is fixed here. That is correct for a transformation function because, with *all* input levels fixed, proportions of ("strict" *or* "broad") joint products are fixed. What the production function (2.1.4) tells us that a transformation function like F^i cannot, is what Buchanan conveys in his isocost curves: the proportion between y_a and y_b can be changed (by altering input combinations).

---

[13] These just represent different two-dimensional slices of the total cost hypersurface than the total cost curve in Figure 2. In Figure 2, q_1 is held constant while in Figure 4, k_1 is held constant.

[14] Actually, $P.O.$ is a mapping from a point in the output space of all the affected firms onto the output plane of Firm 1. We will examine how the point $P.O.$ is found in sections 3.1 and 3.2. The analogous concept in Buchanan's construction is the locus of Pareto optimal points, each point representing a situation which cannot be improved upon by voluntary bargains among the affected parties.

[15] If we wish to apply this to externalities among producers, the "consumption" goods can be one or more saleable goods and one or more externalities imposed on other firms.

Buchanan goes quite a bit farther than the isocost curves of Figure 4 and the transformation function, developing a mathematical statement of Pareto optimality conditions for externalities in consumption. Careful reading of these conditions will disclose a certain degree of symmetry with the Pareto conditions for externalities in production, to be developed in section 3.1; however, his use of a community transformation function implies certain untenable assumptions which will be discussed in section 3.1.

Buchanan draws no conclusions for tax/subsidy schemes from his analysis. Instead, he discusses the possibility of private bargains among the affected individuals. Bargains *can* result in optimal externality levels, but such bargains cannot always (or even usually) be concluded, as I noted in chapter 1 and will develop further in section 5.2. Although Buchanan does occasionally note some drawbacks of private bargains,[16] he does not discuss any alternatives, leaving one with the impression that he believes that what the market (expanded to include bargains) cannot solve, we must just live with.[17]

RELEVANCE OF THE PRODUCTION FUNCTION TO CURRENT ENVIRON-
MENTAL ISSUES. The question of the flexibility of the production function is at the heart of the current debate over ecology and the present level of national production. There are many who say that we must drastically reduce levels of electric power output, for example, in order to reduce environmental pollution to "acceptable" levels. To the extent that this thinking is conditioned by the traditional economic model of exter-nalities, it is overly pessimistic. Of course, the actual reasoning of the pessimistic environmentalists is far more sophisticated than the traditional economic model. Of course smoke pollution can be reduced by changing to nuclear power, but then thermal pollution of water will be increased. Of course direct discharge of sewage into rivers and lakes can be reduced

---

[16] "Trade will tend to take place until the conditions defined by (4A) [first order conditions for Pareto optimality] are met so long as the interacting group remains small, and so long as bargaining difficulties do not delay the attainment of equilibrium." (p. 409.)

[17] He does suggest "pressures for rules changes through the mechanism of 'political trade,'" implying perhaps prohibitive devices (such as zoning) and changes in legal responsibility for the effects of diseconomies or the costs of reducing them, but seem-ingly excluding decentralized incentive changes, like taxes and subsidies. (p. 409.)

by a massive program of construction of treatment plants, but then an increase in eutrophication occurs (in which the treated matter, discharged into bodies of water, stimulates the growth of algae, which crowd out other species). This is "environmental kickback," where an intricate and apparently unstable ecological general equilibrium system[18] will react to the measures taken to reduce one dimension of externality by increasing another dimension.

The optimistic say this situation is not entirely without hope; it is just more complicated than we ever believed. For example, it has been reported that a biological sewage filter has been developed, enabling treated matter to be piped away and used as fertilizer. This kills two birds with one stone. The process results in a decline in the need for chemical fertilizers, a significant pollutant, as well as a reduction in sewage pollution. If the process is more expensive than conventional treatment, it is simply an illustration of a broad joint product formulation, where the production processes available potentially produce several externalities and the aim is to find a way of producing optimal levels of all of them (not just one) at minimum cost. It may be that a biological filter is the way. The most difficult task, that of designing a sufficiently broad production function, is left to the ecologist and the engineer. The economist has the easier job of designing a model that doesn't hamper their efforts.[19] The tax/subsidy system must not encourage producers to create new externalities in trying to reduce old ones. In this case, the tax on externalities must have several components, one for each of the possible externalities resulting from sewage treatment or electricity production.

2.2. Generalized joint product cost functions

As is customary in the theory of the firm, most of the analysis in the following chapters is conducted in terms of cost functions rather than

---

[18] It is the fervent prayer of ecologists that the instability is always local and short-run.

[19] Unless model (2.1.4) is interpreted very broadly, it may need to be expanded to conceptually handle alternative production processes (like nuclear power) that imply a completely different kind of plant. We usually think of a production function as applying to a single method of production (although we modify this somewhat to account for substitution of inputs and for switching of techniques as we adjust plant size to output scale). We may wish to represent completely different processes as additional sets of equations. These will still trace out a total cost curve like Figure 2.

production functions.[20] However, as Samuelson emphasized,[21] cost functions should be derived from input prices and production functions because we have built up a method of analysis and a body of theoretical knowledge about the latter. Thus, we assert that by constrained cost minimization subject to the production function, a set of minimum-cost input combinations can be found for each level of the saleable outputs and the externalities, and that the cost of these efficient input combinations can be written as a general function of the outputs and the externality levels. A rigorous proof (making use of the implicit function theorem and theorems on convexity) that the production function (2.1.4) does imply the cost function (2.2.1) is given in the next few pages. The cost function of a firm producing a set of saleable outputs and a set of externalities and affected by a set of externalities produced by other firms is

$$k_i = k_i(q_i, X_i)$$

where

$$X_i = (X_{i1}, x_{i0m}) \qquad\qquad (m = 1, \ldots, M) \qquad (2.2.1)$$

This cost function presents one major difference when compared with the usual cost functions. Cost is ordinarily stated as a function of outputs alone, assuming that the choice of efficient input combinations has already been made. In this case, however, some of the elements of X_i are inputs to the firm. It is reasonable to treat these as variables, however, because the market provides no prices for these inputs and our ultimate objective is to find and impose a vector of taxes and subsidies which may be interpreted as "prices." So long as these "prices" have not yet been determined, the firm cannot determine efficient combinations of those externalities which are inputs.[22] (In the absence of the expectation of taxes and subsidies or feasible private bargains, the firm could treat the price of externality inputs

---

[20] Since the succeeding chapters will be dealing with optimality and equilibrium proofs, we should think of the production and cost functions as applying to long-run situations. Of course the same notation, with the addition to fixed-cost constants, applies to short-run functions.

[21] *Foundations* (1947), p. 61.

[22] Technically, the way in which we get externality inputs into the cost function is to hold all saleable outputs and all externalities constant in the implicit production function when performing the constrained cost minimization. This guarantees that the only variables in the expansion path function will be the saleable inputs. Inversion will then give q_i and X_i as variables.

as zero, find efficient input combinations, and eliminate externalities from the cost function.)

If we allow first increasing and then decreasing returns to scale for saleable outputs, we get the usual U-shaped average cost curves for saleable outputs. There is no reason to restrict the production function to first-degree homogeneity or some other special shape so long as we assume diminishing returns to a fixed factor and some limit to increasing returns to scale. (Inexhaustible increasing returns to scale would violate our assumption of perfect competition as well as being mathematically embarrassing.)

For two reasons, it seems desirable to derive the cost function from first principles explicitly, rather than simply asserting this can be done. As I have noted, we are introducing a new set of variables (externalities) some of which may be inputs and some outputs, all without market prices. Second, some of the saleable inputs will be "joint inputs." We must show that cost functions can be derived under these assumptions. The reader who is prepared to take on faith my conclusion that the generalized joint product production function, if it is "well behaved," implies the unique, convex cost function (2.2.1), may wish to read lightly the next subsection and then look at the following subsection in which the cost curve is derived by graphical analysis.

DERIVATION OF COST FUNCTION FROM PRODUCTION FUNCTION. We assume that a firm has the set of implicit production functions derived in section 2.1:

$$F_{i1}(q_i, X_{i1}, v_{i1}^n, v_i^p) = 0 \qquad (i = 1, \ldots, R$$

$$F_{ik}(x_{i0m}, v_{ik}^n, v_i^p) = 0 \qquad m = 1, \ldots, M$$

$$v_{in} = \sum_{k=1}^{K} v_{ikn} \qquad \begin{aligned} k &= m + 1 = 2, \ldots, K \quad (2.1.4) \\ n &= 1, \ldots, N) \end{aligned}$$

For given $q_i = \bar{q}_i$, $X_{i1} = \bar{X}_{i1}$, and $x_{i0m} = \bar{x}_{i0m}$, the production set defines isoquants in factor space, which we assume to be strictly convex. Convexity in F_{ik} has the same meaning as in ordinary production functions: diminishing returns to all inputs.[23] However, one must apply "diminishing

---

[23] Note that when we change levels of variables in F_{ik} so as to determine whether it is convex, we ignore the effect on other equations in i's production set of changes in common variables.

returns" carefully when talking about an externality which is a "bad." For an input which can be used to reduce the "bad," diminishing returns means given unit increases of the input result in progressively smaller reductions in the "bad," other inputs constant. For an input which increases the "bad" (a joint input), diminishing returns means given unit increases in the input result in progressively larger increases in the "bad," other inputs constant. The logic of the latter assumption is this: if we have given amounts of filters, precipitators, catalytic agents, smokestacks, etc., limited amounts of sulfur dioxide can be removed from the smoke in a given time period. Additions of sulfur-bearing oil will permit nearly all of the additional SO_2 generated to escape. Convexity of F_{ik} (or positive definiteness of $h'H_{F_2}h$) requires that $\partial^2 F_{ik}/\partial v_{ikn}^2 > 0$, $\partial^2 F_{ik}/\partial v_{ip}^2 > 0$, for all n, p. Hence the necessity of the diminishing returns interpretations above. With a set of input prices w_n $(n = 1, \ldots, N)$ and w_p $(p = 1, \ldots, P)$, we can minimize cost subject to the constraints given by the isoquants

$$C = \sum_{n=1}^{N} \sum_{k=1}^{K} w_n v_{ikn} + \sum_{p=1}^{P} w_p v_{ip} + \lambda_{i1} F_{i1}(q_i, X_{i1}, v_{i1}^n, v_i^p)$$

$$+ \sum_{k=2}^{K} \lambda_{ik} F_{ik}(x_{i0m}, v_{ik}^n, v_i^p) \qquad (2.2.2)$$

The first-order conditions for minimum cost are

$$\frac{\partial C}{\partial v_{ikn}} = w_n + \lambda_{ik} \frac{\partial F_{ik}}{\partial v_{ikn}} = 0 \qquad \begin{matrix} (k = 1, \ldots, K \\ n = 1, \ldots, N)^{24} \end{matrix}$$

$$\frac{\partial C}{\partial v_{ip}} = w_p + \sum_{k=1}^{K} \lambda_{ik} \frac{\partial F_{ik}}{\partial v_{ip}} = 0 \qquad (p = 1, \ldots, P) \qquad (2.2.3)$$

$$\frac{\partial C}{\partial \lambda_{ik}} = F_{ik} = 0 \qquad (k = 1, \ldots, K)$$

Values satisfying these equations (for given $\bar{q}_i$, $\overline{X}_{i1}$, $\bar{x}_{i0m}$) are v_{ikn}^*, v_{ip}^*, λ_{ik}^*. The second-order conditions for minimum cost are: the determinant of

---

[24] We allow k to run from $1, \ldots, K$ for compactness.

the bordered Hessian matrix

$$H_1 = \begin{bmatrix} \dfrac{\partial^2 C}{\partial v_{ikn}^* \, \partial v_{iks}^*} & \dfrac{\partial^2 C}{\partial v_{ikn}^* \, \partial v_{ip}^*} & \dfrac{\partial F_{ik}}{\partial v_{ikn}^*} \\[2ex] \dfrac{\partial^2 C}{\partial v_{iks}^* \, \partial v_{it}^*} & \dfrac{\partial^2 C}{\partial v_{ip}^* \, \partial v_{it}^*} & \dfrac{\partial F_{ik}}{\partial v_{ip}^*} \\[2ex] \dfrac{\partial F_{ik}}{\partial v_{iks}^*} & \dfrac{\partial F_{ik}}{\partial v_{it}^*} & 0 \end{bmatrix}$$

$$= \begin{bmatrix} \lambda_{ik}\dfrac{\partial^2 F_{ik}}{\partial v_{ikn}^* \, \partial v_{iks}^*} & \lambda_{ik}\dfrac{\partial^2 F_{ik}}{\partial v_{ikn}^* \, \partial v_{ip}^*} & \dfrac{\partial F_{ik}}{\partial v_{ikn}^*} \\[2ex] \lambda_{ik}\dfrac{\partial^2 F_{ik}}{\partial v_{is}^* \, \partial v_{it}^*} & \displaystyle\sum_{k=1}^{K} \lambda_{ik}\dfrac{\partial^2 F_{ik}}{\partial v_{ip}^* \, \partial v_{it}^*} & \dfrac{\partial F_{ik}}{\partial v_{ip}^*} \\[2ex] \dfrac{\partial F_{ik}}{\partial v_{iks}^*} & \dfrac{\partial F_{ik}}{\partial v_{it}^*} & 0 \end{bmatrix} \qquad (2.2.4)$$

$$(n, s = 1, \ldots, N; \; p, t = 1, \ldots, P; \; k = 1, \ldots, K)^{25}$$

and all its principal minors, $H_2, \ldots, H_{KN+P-K}$, must be >0 if K is even, <0 if K is odd. We know from a theorem on convexity[26] that, if all F_{ik} are strictly convex, the second-order conditions are satisfied for all v_{ikn}, v_{ip}, and λ_{ik}. Thus the particular values satisfying equations (2.2.3) give a unique minimum.

The cost function states the cost of that combination of inputs which minimizes the cost of producing each output level. That is, it embodies the minimum-cost conditions (2.2.3). We must prove that we can solve (2.2.3) for the inputs as functions of the outputs. Using the input prices, we can

[25] s and t are introduced as additional input subscripts so we may take cross partial derivatives where the two inputs are not the same. Note also that if $K > 1$, 0 in the matrix (2.2.4) is a null matrix, not a scalar.

[26] See property (x) of convex functions, Karlin (1959), II, p. 364. This property was interpreted for the purposes of the present study by a theorem in Samuelson (1947), pp. 376–378, on necessary and sufficient conditions for a quadratic form to be positive definite.

The purpose of deriving the equivalent form of the Hessian (the matrix to the right of the = sign) is to make it easier to see how the theorem on convexity of F_{ik} is applied.

then write the cost of the inputs in place of the input levels, thus arriving at cost as a function of the output levels.

By the implicit function theorem,[27] we can solve equations (2.2.3) for v_{ikn}, v_{ip}, λ_{ik} in terms of q_i, X_{i1}, x_{i0m} if the Jacobian determinant

$$\left| \frac{\partial\left(\frac{\partial C}{\partial v_{ikn}}, \frac{\partial C}{\partial v_{ip}}, \frac{\partial C}{\partial \lambda_{ik}} \right)}{\partial(v_{iks}, v_{it}, \lambda_{iu})} \right| \qquad \begin{array}{l} (n, s = 1, \ldots, N \\ p, t = 1, \ldots, P \\ k, u = 1, \ldots, K) \end{array} \qquad (2.2.5)$$

does not vanish at the point where (2.2.3) is satisfied. It can be shown that the Jacobian (2.2.5) is equal to the determinant of (2.2.4). There are nine types of cross partial derivatives making up (2.2.5). We can illustrate the approach by which equality of (2.2.4) and (2.2.5) may be shown by expanding three of the cross partials which are typical of all the others

(a) $\dfrac{\partial}{\partial v_{iks}}\left(\dfrac{\partial C}{\partial v_{ikn}}\right) = \dfrac{\partial^2 C}{\partial v_{ikn}\,\partial v_{iks}}$

(b) $\dfrac{\partial}{\partial \lambda_{ik}}\left(\dfrac{\partial C}{\partial v_{ip}}\right) = \dfrac{\partial}{\partial \lambda_{ik}}\left(w_p + \sum_{k=1}^{K} \lambda_{ik}\dfrac{\partial F_{ik}}{\partial v_{ip}}\right) = \dfrac{\partial F_{ik}}{\partial v_{ip}}$

(c) $\dfrac{\partial}{\partial \lambda_{ik}}\left(\dfrac{\partial C}{\partial \lambda_{ik}}\right) = \dfrac{\partial}{\partial \lambda_{ik}}(F_{ik}) = 0$

If we expand all of the terms of (2.2.5) in this manner and write them in matrix form, we shall have a matrix identical to (2.2.4). By convexity of the F_{ik}, we know that the second-order conditions are satisfied and, therefore, that the Jacobian (2.2.5) is non-zero.

The implicit function theorem says that functions of the form

$$v_{ikn} = f_{ikn}(\bar{q}_i, \bar{X}_{i1}, \bar{x}_{i0m}) \qquad (n = 1, \ldots, N$$

$$v_{ip} = f_{ip}(\bar{q}_i, \bar{X}_{i1}, \bar{x}_{i0m}) \qquad p = 1, \ldots, P \qquad (2.2.6)$$

$$\lambda_{ik} = f_{ik}(\bar{q}_i, \bar{X}_{i1}, \bar{x}_{i0m}) \qquad k = 1, \ldots, K)$$

[27] See Theorem III, Taylor (1955), p. 249, and exercises 10, 11, p. 253.

39

exist in the neighborhood of a point in the $L + RM$ space of the variables $\bar{q}_i$, $\bar{X}_{i1}$, $\bar{x}_{i0m}$. However, strict convexity assures us that the determinant of (2.2.4) is always $\neq 0$ and therefore the Jacobian (2.2.5) never vanishes. Thus, functions (2.2.6) always exist for all points in $L + RM$ space.[28]

We can substitute the functions defined by (2.2.6) for v_{ikn} and v_{ip} in the cost equation $C = \sum_n \sum_k w_n v_{ikn} + \sum_p w_p v_{ip}$ to get

$$C = \sum_n \sum_k w_n f_{ikn}(q_i, X_{i1}, x_{i0m}) + \sum_p w_p f_{ip}(q_i, X_{i1}, x_{i0m})$$
$$= k_i(q_i, X_i).^{29} \qquad (2.2.1)$$

The expression to the right of the second $=$ sign is the generalized joint product cost function.

GRAPHICAL ANALYSIS. Let us first develop the cost curve for the firm producing an externality. For a firm producing $L + M$ outputs, the cost curve is a surface in $L + M + 1$ dimensions. However, we can take a two-dimensional slice of this hypersurface representing the total cost of producing all outputs as we vary the externality level, holding all the other outputs constant. We shall show how this cost curve may be generated from the production function.

Figure 5 graphs the relevant parts of the production function of a firm (firm 1) which produces the externality x_{101}, and other outputs ($\bar{q}_1$) which are held constant. It uses only two inputs, v_{11n} and v_{1p}, ordinary and joint inputs respectively (or if it has other inputs, we hold them constant, generating only a slice of the complete production set).[30] v_{11n} appears in

[28] The same point can be made in another way. The optimal variable levels, v_{ikn}^*, v_{ip}^*, λ_{ik}^*, are changed as we allow parametric joint product levels, q_i, X_{i1}, x_{i0m}, to change. Any set of input and multiplier levels optimal for some joint product levels will satisfy the corresponding Hessian (evaluated at the particular input, multiplier, and parameter levels) and will therefore give a non-vanishing Jacobian.

[29] We define $X_i = (X_{i1}, x_{i0m}; m = 1, \ldots, M)$ to include all externalities produced and received by i. This is possible because, in the single-equation cost function, we no longer have to put externalities received by the firm in one equation and externalities produced by it in another.

[30] Note that Figure 5 represents the entire production set not just one equation. It can be derived by mapping constant q_1 points from surfaces (in the appropriate spaces) representing F_{11} and F_{12} onto $v_{11n} - v_{1p} - x_{101}$ space. If these surfaces conform to the diminishing returns assumptions noted earlier, the shape of curve shown in Figure 5 will result.

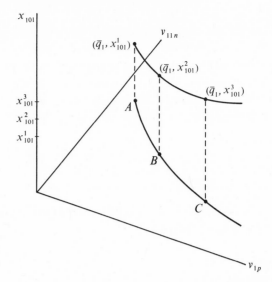

FIGURE 5

Production function of a firm

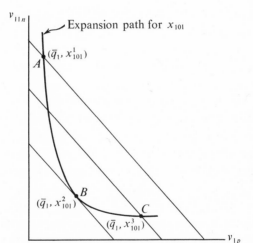

FIGURE 6

Expansion path

F_{11} and v_{1p} appears in F_{11} and in F_{12} (the production equation in which x_{101} appears). Since v_{1p} is the only argument of F_{12} which is allowed to vary, the isoquant for a particular level of x_{101} is a point. That is, each level of v_{1p} implies one and only one level of x_{101} (other outputs constant). Therefore, there is no choice to be made among different input combinations as we increase x_{101}. The expansion path for x_{101} is predetermined and

41

independent of relative input prices.[31] Figure 5 shows this expansion path in three dimensions and its mapping onto the $v_{11n} - v_{1p}$ plane. Three successively higher levels of x_{101} are labeled A, B, and C. The mapping of the expansion path onto the $v_{11n} - v_{1p}$ plane is repeated in Figure 6 and a set of relative prices imposed. The level of total cost at each point along the expansion path is given by the total cost associated with the isocost line

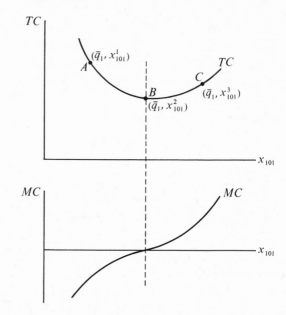

FIGURE 7

Total and marginal cost curves

passing through that point. We can see from the height of the isocost lines the total cost of points A, B, and C. Total cost is then plotted in Figure 7.

Only the cost curve on one side of the minimum-cost point (point B in Figure 7) is usually of interest in a given problem. For an electrical utility using "dirty" fuel, the part of the TC curve to the right of B implies

[31] If we have more variable inputs, say two ordinary inputs appearing in F_{11}, *and* v_{1p}, there may be an efficiency choice to be made among input levels. However, it is still true that for a given level of x_{101} only one level of v_{1p} is possible. The only choice made is between levels of the other inputs. If we also allow an input appearing in F_{12} (the equation of firm 1's production set in which x_{101} appears) to vary, we may then vary v_{1p}. But we must also vary an input in *each* of the equations of the production set. To sum it up, the introduction of a joint input gives us one less degree of freedom in making the efficiency choice. Any three-dimensional slice of the production surface involving v_{1p}, x_{101}, and an ordinary input will look like Figure 5 to the extent of having a $\bar{q}_1$ isoquant curve rather than a surface.

allocating some fuel solely for the purpose of producing pollution. This part of the curve is of interest only if x_{101} is an external economy and we are considering paying the firm to increase its production of it.

A special case of this general shape of TC is where point B is on the TC axis, that is, the cost curve is always upward-sloping. The externality is only a potential one and production will always be zero unless it is paid for.

The upturn in TC is a consequence of the assumption that there is a limit to the amount of the joint input(s) that can be used efficiently in the production of any *given* amount of outputs. (That is, we are making the standard assumption of diminishing returns to any input in the production of a saleable output.) To increase x_{101} production beyond the level implied by the efficient use of joint inputs requires allocating inputs just for that purpose. It is costly, just as producing any output is costly.

To a firm minimizing cost, the level of x_{101} is irrelevant. Then the expansion path pictured in Figures 5 and 6 is, for that firm, simply a $\bar{q}_1$ isoquant. Its shape is therefore a consequence of diminishing returns or the diminishing rate of technical substitution between the two inputs. This shape, then, implies the shape of the cost curve. (The firm only cares about one point on the cost curve, point B, corresponding to the point where the lowest isocost line touches the $\bar{q}_1$ isoquant.) The absence of local minima in TC other than the global minimum is a consequence of the standard assumption that the rate of technical substitution between the inputs is always diminishing.

If we change the (constant) level of some other output, we must take another two-dimensional slice of the cost hypersurface. This could be plotted on Figure 7.[32] Now, of course, if firm 1 is maximizing its profit independently, it will choose that level of x_{101} which minimizes its cost of producing the saleable output, point B in Figure 7. The locus of such points as we change the level of the other output (this locus is labeled "k_j *min*" in Figure 2, section 2.1) traces out the possible externality levels in the absence of government intervention or private bargains to alter the externality level.

Marginal cost is shown in the lower panel of Figure 7. Whenever two or more outputs are produced in a single production process, we must be

---

[32] If the cost function is separable [$k_1(q_1, x_{101}) = k_{11}(q_1) + k_{12}(x_{101})$], every two-dimensional slice will have the same shape and position vis-à-vis the x_{101} axis; only the height above the x_{101} axis will differ.

careful about interpretations and allocations of cost. Thus we may interpret marginal cost as the change in the total cost of producing x_{101} and given levels of all other outputs, as x_{101} changes. An average cost derived by dividing total cost by x_{101} would be misleading and we can get along without it.

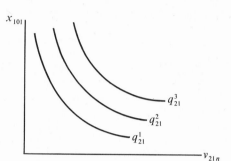

FIGURE 8

Isoquants for firm receiving external economy

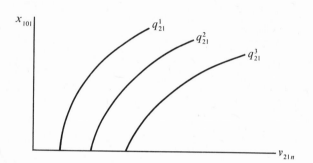

FIGURE 9

Isoquants for firm receiving external diseconomy

Now we must depict the cost curves of a firm *receiving* an externality. (Let us call the externality x_{101} and the recipient firm 2. As before, we shall hold the output(s) of the firm constant, thus taking two-dimensional slices of the production and cost functions.) The shape of the curves depends on whether the externality is an economy or a diseconomy. We can see this first by comparing firm 2's isoquants when an input is an external economy with the case where an input is an external diseconomy. (Figures 8 and 9.)

Let us deal first with Figure 8 where x_{101} is an *external economy*. If firm 2 is free to choose the levels it desires of all inputs including the externality, Figure 8 shows its input substitution possibilities. Of course it is not free to choose externality levels, so what the diagram actually portrays is information it would need in trying to make bargains with the externality

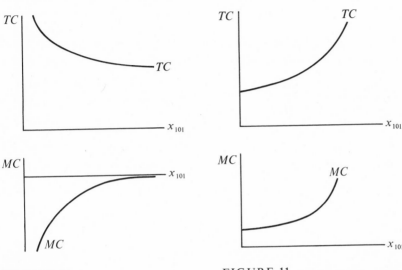

FIGURE 10
Total and marginal cost curves for firm receiving external economy

FIGURE 11
Total and marginal cost curves for firm receiving external diseconomy

producer to alter his behavior. It will be shown in chapter 3 that this information is quite relevant to finding and enforcing Pareto efficient externality levels. The shape of the isoquants is quite standard. They embody the assumption of diminishing returns to increasing amounts of a fixed factor, whether that factor be an ordinary input or an externality. As x_{101} increases, it takes less and less of input v_{21n} (other inputs, if any, held constant) to maintain a constant level of the (one, for simplicity) saleable output q_{21}. Thus, total cost of producing that output level must fall. Figure 10 shows the resulting total cost curve. The same shape will obtain when there are several inputs which are allowed to vary. Figure 10 then depicts the cost of efficient input combinations capable of producing

45

given levels of all outputs as x_{101} varies, allowing all other inputs to vary optimally.[33]

MC is negative throughout but rising due to the convexity of TC. The average derived by dividing TC by the level of x_{101} does not seem to be capable of meaningful interpretation, and so is omitted.

The cost curves for a firm receiving an external *diseconomy* are shown in Figure 11. They embody the assumption that the amount of extra costly input required per unit increase of the externality increases as x_{101} increases.[34] This assumption of convex isoquants implies that the locus of efficient costly input combinations as x_{101} increases is convex and therefore that the cost function is convex. With TC convex and upward-sloping, MC is always positive and upward-sloping.

Should x_{101} be an economy at first and then a diseconomy, we can see from Figures 10 and 11 together that the recipient firm's TC curve would be U-shaped. Its minimum point would of course not necessarily correspond with the minimum point of the producer's TC.

[33] To spare your having to look at another three-dimensional diagram, let me help you imagine one. Assume three inputs, one of them an externality, with the isoquant surface convex to the origin. The locus of minimum-cost combinations of ordinary inputs capable of producing given outputs as we increase x_{101} is a curve along that isoquant surface. That curve is therefore convex to the origin. Its mapping onto the plane of ordinary inputs associates a lower cost (a budget line with smaller v_1 and v_2 intercepts) with each higher level of x_1.

If one of the inputs is a joint input (which firm 2 uses in producing a saleable output and an externality *it* imposes on others), the choice of efficient input combinations is slightly more constrained. Firm 2 *can* vary the level of the joint input and still hold all output levels constant, but it must adjust several other inputs to do so since the joint input appears in several equations of the production set. Naturally, it will make these adjustments if that lowers its cost.

[34] This is equivalent to an assumption of diminishing returns. Reducing a "bad" is similar to increasing a "good." So we assume that as x_{101} falls, other inputs constant, a smaller and smaller increase of firm 2's saleable output results. This determines the curvature of the isoquants in Figure 9.

The assumption of diminishing returns, as applied to the input of an external diseconomy, is critically re-examined in section 4.6.

THREE

PARETO OPTIMALITY IN THE MODEL OF GENERALIZED JOINT PRODUCTION

3.1. Conditions for achieving Pareto efficiency when externalities are present

Previous works on production externalities have always assumed that socially optimal outputs are those which maximize combined profit of the firms affected by the externalities, without seeking to justify this assumption in terms of the fundamental tools of analysis of modern price and welfare theory. Perhaps for this reason the theory of externalities has remained outside the core of economic theory and is mentioned in textbooks more as an exception to "the principles" than as a part of them. This section will derive efficiency conditions for production externalities,[1] and the next section will show that outputs which maximize combined profit meet these conditions.

The fundamental theorem of welfare economics holds that if N consumers and R firms each act as perfect competitors and maximize their individual utility and profit respectively, the result is optimal in the Pareto sense. (No increase in one consumer's utility can be made without reducing some other consumer's utility; no increase in one commodity can be made without reducing some other commodity, given resource levels.) If, however, some or all of the R firms experience production externalities, their outputs will not all meet the Pareto criterion. This has been asserted

---

[1] The need for developing such conditions was pointed out by Professors Lancaster and Wellisz.

in previous works on production externalities and it will be demonstrated in Appendix A by direct application of the test for Pareto efficiency to be derived in this section. The N consumers are not (by definition) affected by the technological externalities linking the firms. Thus, maximizing individual utility given the outputs of the firms, they will satisfy the Pareto criteria. It is our task in this section to derive the conditions under which the outputs of the R firms will also be Pareto efficient.

Efficiency in production must be carefully defined for an economy of R firms, each of which produces (in general) several commodities which may be produced by other firms as well. Following Lange (1942) we shall take an efficient point to be a point where we cannot increase the total output of one commodity without reducing the total output of some other commodity or increasing the total quantity of some input, that is, a point on society's production possibility frontier. This definition of efficiency does not necessarily imply holding constant the outputs of any firms.[2] In a Pareto framework, we are concerned with the output levels of individual firms only as they affect profit (or net rent) and in turn affect the utility of individuals having ownership shares in firms. Applying the Pareto criterion in the consumer sector guarantees that no change in a firm's output will hurt any individual. If (as here) we do not solve the Pareto conditions simultaneously for the consumption sector, we implicitly assume either that compensation is made to individuals hurt by changes in any firm's outputs or inputs or that such a redistribution of income is acceptable under our welfare criterion. *Any* method of correcting a violation of the Pareto conditions (e.g., eliminating monopolies) is likely to involve such a redistribution of income.

To find an efficient point, we shall maximize the total output of one commodity while holding constant the total amounts of all other saleable commodities and costly inputs. The externalities (elements of X_i) will be allowed to vary since they affect cost and profit of any firm only as they

---

[2] If we increase one output of one firm while holding all other outputs of that firm and other firms constant, we may still not arrive at a point on society's production possibility frontier. A further reallocation of the fixed total quantity of all inputs may increase some firms' outputs of a particular commodity more than it reduces other firms' output of that commodity. Henderson and Quandt (1958) make the mistake of formulating their multi-product, multi-firm optimality conditions in this way (see pp. 205–206). Other textbook treatments skirt the problem by dealing with special cases where one firm is the only producer of a commodity.

48

value of each of the variables that maximizes q_{11}. This solution naturally embodies the specific constraint set, (3.1.10). What we really want, however, is the set of efficiency conditions that tells us how to allocate any possible resource endowment. That is, we want to try different fixed levels of the inputs and trace out the locus of efficient points. This we do by simply dropping the constraint set, (3.1.10). The remaining first-order conditions must hold for there to be an efficient allocation of any resource endowment. There is no reason to expect the Lagrange multipliers which appear in equation sets (3.1.5) to (3.1.9) to remain the same when the constraints change, however. Thus, to have a set of conditions which are completely independent of the constraints, it is desirable to eliminate the multipliers. It happens that this also makes possible a very interesting interpretation of the Pareto conditions.

First, let us eliminate the multipliers from the conditions involving (one) particular ordinary input, v_n (whose components are the $v_{ikn}, i = 1, \ldots, R$; $k = 1, \ldots, K$), and (one) particular externality, x_{j0m}. The equations involving v_{ikn} ($R K$ or fewer equations in [3.1.7] above) and x_{j0m} (one equation in [3.1.9] above) are a subset of the conditions, so we should expect our result to be just one of a number of conditions which must hold simultaneously.

Our approach is to substitute expressions involving the v_{ikn} for the multipliers in the equation $\partial Q / \partial x_{j0m}$. So first we solve for λ_{ik} the equations in (3.1.7) involving v_{ikn}:

$$\lambda_{ik} = \frac{\mu_n}{\partial F_{ik} / \partial v_{ikn}} \qquad \begin{matrix} (i = 1, \ldots, R \\ k = 1, \ldots, K) \end{matrix}$$

Now if input n does not appear in a particular F_{ik}, there will be no equation in (3.1.7) involving v_{ikn}, so we cannot solve for λ_{ik} in this manner. Let us say that one (it could be more—the approach is perfectly general) of the multipliers we wish to substitute for cannot be written in this way. Call it λ_{r1} and let it remain in the equations $\partial Q / \partial x_{j0m}$. Substitute for the rest of the multipliers

$$\begin{aligned} \frac{\partial Q}{\partial x_{j0m}} = {} & \frac{\partial F_{jk} / \partial x_{j0m}}{\partial F_{jk} / \partial v_{jkn}} \cdot \mu_n \\ & + \sum_{\substack{i=1 \\ i \neq j \neq r}}^{R} \frac{\partial F_{i1} / \partial x_{j0m}}{\partial F_{i1} / \partial v_{i1n}} \cdot \mu_n + \lambda_{r1} \frac{\partial F_{r1}}{\partial x_{j0m}} = 0 \end{aligned} \qquad (3.1.11)$$

51

Next, we take the total derivative with respect to x_{j0m} of each of the production functions in the equation above, applying the implicit function rule. Since we hold all variables except v_n and x_{j0m} constant when we derive *ceteris paribus* substitution conditions between these two, only the derivatives with respect to these variables are non-zero. The derivatives are

$$\frac{dF_{jk}}{dx_{j0m}} = \frac{\partial F_{jk}}{\partial x_{j0m}} + \frac{\partial F_{ik}}{\partial v_{jkn}} \cdot \frac{\partial v_{jkn}}{\partial x_{j0m}} = 0$$

$$\frac{dF_{i1}}{dx_{j0m}} = \frac{\partial F_{i1}}{\partial x_{j0m}} + \frac{\partial F_{i1}}{\partial v_{i1n}} \cdot \frac{\partial v_{i1n}}{\partial x_{j0m}} = 0$$

$$\frac{dF_{r1}}{dx_{j0m}} = \frac{\partial F_{r1}}{\partial x_{j0m}} = 0$$

$$(i = 1, \ldots, R; \neq j, r)$$

The last equation in the set above tells us that the last term in (3.1.10) falls out. The other equations can all be solved in a manner that we shall just illustrate for the first of them:

$$\frac{\partial v_{jkn}}{\partial x_{j0m}} = -\frac{\partial F_{jk}/\partial x_{j0m}}{\partial F_{jk}/\partial v_{jkn}}$$

Substituting these expressions in (3.1.11), taking out the common factor μ_n,[5] and rearranging terms, we get

$$\frac{\partial v_{jkn}}{\partial x_{j0m}} = -\sum_{\substack{i=1 \\ i \neq j,r}}^{R} \frac{\partial v_{i1n}}{\partial x_{j0m}} \qquad \begin{aligned} &(n = 1, \ldots, N \\ &m = 1, \ldots, M \\ &j = 1, \ldots, R) \end{aligned} \qquad (3.1.12)$$

Because we can choose *any* ordinary input and *any* externality for this multiplier-eliminating operation, we can say that (3.1.12) holds for any input, v_n $(n = 1, \ldots, N)$, combined with any externality, x_{j0m} $(j = 1, \ldots, R; m = 1, \ldots, M)$. Naturally, in a Pareto optimum all these conditions hold simultaneously.

[5] μ_n must not be zero. If μ_n were zero, we could not remove it from (3.1.11) and be sure that the remaining expressions summed to zero. We know from the theory of Lagrange multipliers (see Hadley [1964], p. 73, for proof) that $\mu_n = \partial Q/\partial v_n$. This derivative is zero only if an increase in v_n will not increase the output q_{11}. This would mean that the input is available in greater supply than all the firms together can possibly use. In this case, the input is a free good and we do not need to worry about rules for allocating it.

A similar operation will enable us to eliminate the multipliers from the conditions involving (one) particular joint input, v_p, and (one) particular externality, x_{j0m}. First we solve for λ_{ik} the equations in (3.1.8) involving v_{ip}:

$$\lambda_{ik} = \gamma_p - \frac{\sum\limits_{s=1}^{K,\neq k} \lambda_{is}(\partial F_{is}/\partial v_{ip})}{\partial F_{ik}/\partial v_{ip}} \qquad \begin{array}{l} (i = 1, \ldots, R \\ k = 1, \ldots, K) \end{array}$$

Assume that input p does not appear in production function F_{r1}. λ_{r1} will therefore have to remain in the equation $\partial Q/\partial x_{j0m}$. Substitute for the rest of the multipliers

$$\frac{\partial Q}{\partial x_{j0m}} = \frac{\partial F_{jk}/\partial x_{j0m}}{\partial F_{jk}/\partial v_{jp}}\left[\gamma_p - \sum_{s=1}^{K,\neq k} \lambda_{js}(\partial F_{js}/\partial v_{jp})\right]$$

$$+ \sum_{\substack{i=1 \\ i\neq j,r}}^{R} \frac{\partial F_{i1}/\partial x_{j0m}}{\partial F_{i1}/\partial v_{ip}}\left[\gamma_p - \sum_{s=2}^{K} \lambda_{is}(\partial F_{is}/\partial v_{ip})\right]$$

$$+ \lambda_{r1}\frac{\partial F_{r1}}{\partial x_{j0m}} = 0 \qquad (3.1.13)$$

Taking the derivative with respect to x_{j0m} of each implicit production function in (3.1.13), solving for expressions involving the partial derivative of the input with respect to the externality, substituting in (3.1.13), taking out the common factor γ_p, and rearranging terms, we get

$$\frac{\partial v_{jp}}{\partial x_{j0m}} = -\sum_{\substack{i=1 \\ i\neq j,r}}^{R} \frac{\partial v_{ip}}{\partial x_{j0m}} \qquad \begin{array}{l} (p = 1, \ldots, P \\ m = 1, \ldots, M \\ j = 1, \ldots, R) \end{array} \qquad (3.1.14)$$

Equations sets (3.1.12) and (3.1.14) represent necessary conditions which must hold simultaneously for Pareto efficiency in the presence of externalities. Note that these conditions, being free of the input constraints, define efficient allocation of *any* resource endowment. An equation of (3.1.12), for example, maps the locus of efficient combinations of a level of output x_{j0m} and an allocation of input v_n when we allow the other outputs and inputs to vary. It states that the rate at which the nth input must be used by firm j to produce the mth externality, x_{j0m}, must equal the sum of the marginal rates of substitution between the nth input and the mth externality over all the firms "consuming" the externality.

One can derive multiplier-free conditions for other combinations of variables in (3.1.4), such as any two inputs (ordinary, joint, or mixed), two outputs, or an output and an input. Some of these are familiar (for example, *MPP* of input n in the production of output l must be the same for all firms) and some apply specifically to joint inputs (the sum over k of the *MRS* of an ordinary input for a joint input must be equal for all firms). The two conditions we present explicitly seem to be the most interesting.

Equations sets (3.1.12) and (3.1.14) are analogous to the well-known Samuelson efficiency conditions for public consumption goods. These conditions are embodied in Samuelson's equation (2) which in notation consistent with that used in this monograph is[6]

$$\sum_i \left[\frac{\partial u_i}{\partial X_{n+j}} \bigg/ \frac{\partial u_i}{\partial X_r} \right] = \frac{\partial F}{\partial X_{n+j}} \bigg/ \frac{\partial F}{\partial X_r} \qquad \begin{aligned} &(i = 1, \ldots, s \\ &\ j = 1, \ldots, m \\ &\ r = 1, \ldots, n) \end{aligned}$$

where

X_{n+j} is the jth collective consumption good.

X_r is the rth private consumption good.

$F(X_1, \ldots, X_{n+m})$ is a production possibility schedule relating totals of all outputs, public and private.

u_i is the utility of the ith individual.

This equation, as Samuelson interprets it, "makes relative marginal social cost [units of the private good given up to produce one unit of the public good] equal to the sum of all persons' marginal rates of substitution [of the private good for the public good]."[7] In my (3.1.12) v_n is a private good which is an input to the production process. $\partial v_{jkn}/\partial x_{j0m}$ represents the rate at which the valuable private good n must be used to produce the public good x_{j0m}, or the marginal social cost of producing x_{j0m}. Equation (3.1.12) shows this to be equal to the sum of the marginal rates of substitution between the private good and the public good for all firms "consuming" both in their production process. The same interpretation can be made for the joint input v_p.

This result is not too surprising since we have treated externalities as public producers' goods. It would appear that the conditions for externalities should extend to other public producers' goods. If so, they would be

---

[6] Samuelson (1954), p. 387.

[7] Samuelson (1955), p. 353. I have added the bracketed phrases.

of somewhat more general applicability than we have claimed, and a more complete analogue to Samuelson's conditions.

It should be noted here that Buchanan and Stubblebine (1962), Buchanan (1966), and Mishan (1969) have all stated optimality conditions for externalities involving summation over individuals. We cannot directly compare any of these results with the results here because all treat externalities among consumers and use different production and transformation functions for the externality producer. Of the three, only Buchanan and Stubblebine use a production function and it is of the multi-product type (2.1.1) and not of the generalized joint product type. The more recent articles use transformation functions. All firms are lumped together in such a community transformation function (remember that a firm producing externalities has a point transformation function; only when we lump them together and obscure the input allocations within and among firms do we get a curve). As Lange (1942)[8] points out, a community transformation function implicitly assumes all firms have identical transformation functions. When, as is often the case, this assumption is not justified, the form of the transformation function interdepends with the quantities of inputs used by and the quantities of outputs produced by each firm. In other words, the use of a community transformation function between q_i and x_m (for example) assumes the greatest q_i is produced for each level of x_m (with given total quantities of inputs); it *assumes* optimal resource allocation. If a community transformation function is assumed for the production sector when the optimal level of externalities affecting consumers is determined, there is no assurance that optimal allocation within the production sector will actually come about. If it is assumed in a model of the production sector alone, it entirely begs the question of deriving conditions for such an optimal resource allocation and enforcing optimality. A complete approach to production sector optimality or production and consumption sector optimality must begin with the production functions of firms.

GRAPHICAL EXPOSITION OF EFFICIENCY CONDITIONS. Let us first develop a diagrammatic version of conditions (3.1.12), showing efficient allocation of *ordinary inputs*. To be concrete, let us take a three-firm case where firm 3 produces a public good external *diseconomy*, x_{301}, of which

[8] Lange (1942), p. 224.

firms 1 and 2 are recipients. An ordinary input, v_n, may be used by firm 3 to reduce the externality (if it has any incentive to do so) and by 1 and 2 to increase production of their saleable outputs. Starting from an initial allocation of inputs among the firms and resulting output levels (which we may think of as the market solution where each firm maximizes profit without consideration of the effect on other firms), our goal is to increase one output, say q_1, without reducing any other output. All inputs must be reallocated to accomplish this, but we shall concentrate on one, v_n.

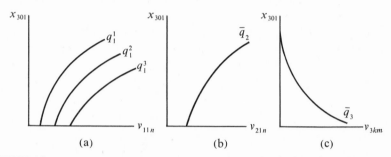

FIGURE 12

Production functions of three firms affected by an external diseconomy

The producer's total product (of externality) curve was represented as Figure 3, panel (b), in chapter 2. It is reproduced here as panel (c) of Figure 12 for completeness.

Firm 1's isoquant map for the inputs x_{301} and v_{11n} is represented in Figure 12, panel (a). As the externality is increased, it takes more of v_{11n} to maintain a constant level of the saleable output, hence the positive slope. Convexity of the production function is implied by the reasonable assumption that for unit increases in the externality, it takes progressively larger increases in the input to keep q_1 constant.

Firm 2's isoquant (for the output, $\bar{q}_2$, which we wish to keep constant) has the same shape as that of firm 1, and we represent it in panel (b).

Because of the public good character of the externality, we can add horizontally the isoquants for firms 1 and 2. A particular level of the externality implies that a particular amount of input n must be allocated to 1 and 2 together in order to keep q_1 and q_2 at constant levels. Because we wish to maximize q_1 while holding q_2 constant, we shall add firm 1's isoquant map to the single $\bar{q}_2$ isoquant.

Open-topped Edgeworth Box. We can make a variant of the Edgeworth box diagram by summing the isoquants of the recipient firms in panels (a) and (b), flipping the producer's total product curve in panel (c) over in space, and superimposing it on the summed isoquants, to get Figure 13. A fixed quantity of input n must be allocated among the three firms, so what firm 3 uses is subtracted from the total to get the balance available for 1 and 2. Because firms 1 and 2 use the amount of the externality produced by 3, their origin must be at the opposite side of the bottom of the box from 3's origin, instead of at opposite corners as in a standard Edgeworth box. The box is open-topped because x_{301} is not constrained.

If the firm minimized cost in isolation, firm 3 would select point I where it wastes no v_n on reducing the externality level. This leaves the total amount of input n to be divided among firms 1 and 2. Given the externality level, q_1^1 is the greatest amount of firm 1's output that can be produced while keeping $\bar{q}_2$ constant. Point $P.O.$ is clearly superior, since with the same total amount of v_n the same amounts of q_3 and q_2 are produced and a higher amount of q_1 is produced. (Of course, this will cost firm 3 more, but we shall show in section 3.2 that combined profit is increased by this reallocation, and therefore the gainers could compensate firm 3.)

$P.O.$ in Figure 13 represents the single point in $x_{30m} - v_n$ space which would satisfy equations (3.1.5) to (3.1.10). If we performed the same operation but held q_3 constant at a different level, we would find another efficient point where a $\bar{q}_2 + q_1$ isoquant is tangent to the new q_3 isoquant. The equation in (3.1.12) involving x_{301} and v_n gives the locus of all such points as we vary the isoquants continuously. This same locus is represented in Figure 14. The efficiency locus gives the (infinite number of) Pareto efficient points as we vary q_3, maximizing q_1.

Now we must develop a graphical version of one equation of conditions (3.1.14), showing efficient allocation of a *joint input*. Assume that firm 1 produces a public good external *economy*, x_{10m}, of which firms 2 and 3 are recipients. The joint input, v_p, is used by all three firms to produce saleable outputs, and produces externalities as by-products. Starting from an initial allocation of inputs among the firms and resulting output levels, our goal is to increase one output, say q_3, without reducing any other output.

57

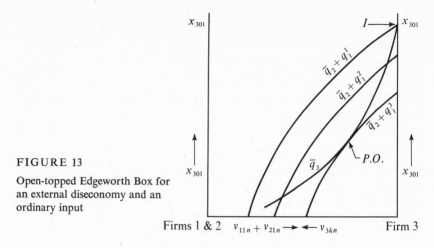

FIGURE 13

Open-topped Edgeworth Box for an external diseconomy and an ordinary input

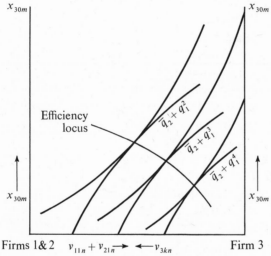

FIGURE 14

Efficiency locus in open-topped Edgeworth Box

We cannot reallocate the joint input alone without reallocating at least one other input because when the joint input changes alone, saleable outputs and some externalities also change. We cannot permit this in a Pareto optimum operation. We shall consider the simplest case where it is only necessary to change one other input.

The relevant part of the production function of the *producer* of the external economy is shown in panel (a) of Figure 15. The relation between the two inputs, v_{2p} and v_{11n}, and the externality, x_{10m}, is shown as the curve in three-dimensional space, labeled AB. As we increase v_{1p}, x_{10m} rises. However, because v_{1p} is also used in producing q_1, if we are to keep q_1 constant, we must decrease v_{11n}, an input used in producing q_1. The dashed lines are projections of AB onto two dimensions. Thus AD is an "iso-quant" for the two inputs where one output quantity, that of x_{10m}, is not held constant. EF is the projection onto the space of the externality and the ordinary input, showing that as the externality increases (because of increases in v_{1p}) v_{11n} must be reduced, so as to keep q_1 constant. Finally, CB is the most important projection for our purposes. It is the "total product"

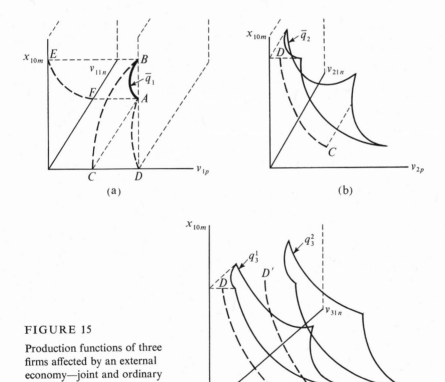

FIGURE 15

Production functions of three firms affected by an external economy—joint and ordinary inputs

59

(of externality) curve for the joint input, when v_{11n} is allowed to vary. (If v_{11n} were not allowed to vary, the total product curve would be a point.) The slope of this curve is given by the derivative, $\partial v_{1p}/\partial x_{10m}$, in the relevant equation of (3.1.13). That one equation considers only the equation F_{1k} $(k = m + 1)$ from firm 1's production set. Nothing about taking that partial derivative prohibits variation in v_{11n} which is a variable in F_{11}.

Look next at firm 2, which is a recipient of the external economy. As the level of the externality falls, more v_{2p} is needed to maintain q_2 constant. Now, to keep the dimensionality within bound, we shall assume that firm 2 produces no externality with v_{2p}. We still have one other variable to account for, however. We saw that when firm 1 uses more v_{1p} and increases the externality, less v_{11n} is needed. Since the Pareto optimum operation allocates a fixed quantity of v_n among the firms, more will be available for firm 2. Panel (b) shows a q_2 isoquant in the space of the three variables, v_{2p}, v_{21n}, and x_{10m}. Now if we hold v_{21n} constant at a particular level, we get a set of unique x_{102} and v_{2p} values. This is the projection CD. It is unlike firm 1's CB projection because the other input is held constant here. A different fixed value of the input would generate a different projection. This is a consequence of the fact that the q_2 isoquant is a surface in three dimensions rather than a curve.

We assume that firm 3's situation is similar to that of firm 2. Firm 3's output, q_3, is the one we have chosen to increase in the Pareto operation, so panel (c) portrays two isoquants. For a fixed level of v_{31n}, the first isoquant gives the projection CD. For a (possibly different) fixed level of v_{31n}, the higher isoquant gives another projection, $C'D'$.

Now we have all the ingredients for a three-dimensional open-topped Edgeworth box but one: the capacity to draw it so it is comprehensible. We shall, instead, concentrate on the projections onto $v_p - x_{102}$ space, drawing just the outlines of the box in three dimensions. In Figure 16 we have put firm 2 and firm 3's origin at the opposite corner of the bottom of the box from firm 1's because both inputs are fixed in quantity and must be allocated between firms which compete for their use.

Point I represents an initial, non-Pareto-optimal situation. It could be a market equilibrium where each firm maximizes profit individually. Each firm is producing its profit-maximizing level of output, using the least cost combination of inputs. Thus firm 1 is using that combination of v_{1p} and

v_{11n} which produces $\bar{q}_1$ at least cost regardless of the resulting level of the externality. Each of the other firms maximizes profit, and the resulting output levels are $\bar{q}_2$ and q_3^1. Thus the projection labeled $\bar{q}_2 + q_3^1$ assumes that the particular levels of v_{21n} and v_{31n} which give it are cost-minimizing levels. Then the levels of v_{2p} and v_{3p} implied by the level of x_{102} and the projection are also cost-minimizing levels. The sum of these amounts of

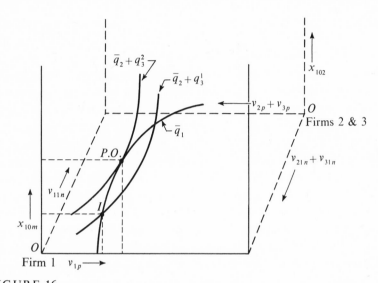

FIGURE 16

Open-topped Edgeworth Box for an external economy and a joint input

each firm's inputs determines the size of the Edgeworth box. We shall now reallocate these inputs so as to increase q_3 without reducing q_1 and q_2.[9]

The point *P.O.* is a Pareto optimal reallocation. Firm 1 has been required to use more v_p so as to produce more x_{102}. This releases some v_n, which may now be used by the other firms. They have less v_p but more x_{102} and v_n. Firm 2 uses no more v_n than is needed to keep q_2 constant, so a great deal more is available for firm 3. The reallocation of v_p continued until the reduction in firm 3's v_{3p} hurt q_3 production more than the increase

[9] Note that the new projection, labeled $\bar{q}_2 + q_3^2$, represents a higher fixed level of v_{31n} and a higher or lower level of v_{21n} depending on the strength of the external economy's effect on $\bar{q}_2$ production.

in x_{102} and v_{31n} together helped it. Equations (3.1.14) tell us that this occurred at point $P.O.$ In three dimensions this represents the tangency of firm 1's production function curve with the summed isoquants of firms 2 and 3. This tangency determines optimum values of the three variables. Taking the optimum value of v_n as a constant, we can project the summed isoquant onto two dimensions. This gives us the curve labeled $\bar{q}_2 + q_3^2$.

3.2. Proof that the rule "maximize combined profit" meets the Pareto efficiency conditions

This section will justify the conventional rule for setting externality levels. We shall show that saleable output and externality levels which maximize combined profit of the group of firms subject to externalities also meet the Pareto efficiency conditions of the previous section. No firm directly affected by an externality of one of the firms in the group can be left out of the group, even if it does not itself produce an externality.[10] We assume, as before, that each of the firms is a perfect competitor on all markets. Now we must treat the group of firms *as if* it were a perfect competitor. That is, even if the group could exercise some degree of monopoly power, we shall make the profit computation using the given market prices faced by each individual firm. This is permissible since the group of firms will never actually merge; the final output and price decisions will be decentralized.

We shall calculate the profit function of one firm as net revenue constrained by the production function (2.1.4). Combined profit is simply the sum over i of the profit functions of the firms:

$$\sum P_i = \sum_{l=1}^{L} p_l \left(\sum_{i=1}^{R} q_{il} \right) - \sum_{n=1}^{N} w_n \left(\sum_{i=1}^{R} \sum_{k=1}^{K} v_{ikn} \right) - \sum_{p=1}^{P} w_p \left(\sum_{i=1}^{R} v_{ip} \right)$$
$$+ \sum_{i=1}^{R} \sum_{k=1}^{K} \lambda_{ik} F_{ik} \tag{3.2.1}$$

All variables and parameters and the production function are defined as in earlier sections. The only new element is the output prices, p_l. The

---

[10] Of course firms affected only through the price of an input are recipients only of a pecuniary externality and should be left out.

first-order conditions for a maximum of net revenue are

$$\frac{\partial \sum P_i}{\partial q_{il}} = p_l + \lambda_{i1}\frac{\partial F_{i1}}{\partial q_{il}} = 0 \qquad \begin{aligned}(i &= 1, \ldots, R \\ l &= 1, \ldots, L)\end{aligned} \qquad (3.2.2)$$

$$\frac{\partial \sum P_i}{\partial v_{ikn}} = -w_n + \lambda_{ik}\frac{\partial F_{ik}}{\partial v_{ikn}} = 0 \qquad \begin{aligned}(i &= 1, \ldots, R \\ k &= 1, \ldots, K \\ n &= 1, \ldots, N)\end{aligned} \qquad (3.2.3)$$

$$\frac{\partial \sum P_i}{\partial v_{ip}} = -w_p + \sum_{k=1}^{K}\lambda_{ik}\frac{\partial F_{ik}}{\partial v_{ip}} = 0 \qquad \begin{aligned}(i &= 1, \ldots, R \\ p &= 1, \ldots, P)\end{aligned} \qquad (3.2.4)$$

$$\frac{\partial \sum P_i}{\partial x_{j0m}} = \lambda_{jk}\frac{\partial F_{jk}}{\partial x_{j0m}} + \sum_{i=1}^{R \neq j}\lambda_{i1}\frac{\partial F_{i1}}{\partial x_{j0m}} \qquad \begin{aligned}(j &= 1, \ldots, R \\ m &= 1, \ldots, M \\ k &= m + 1)\end{aligned}$$
$$= 0 \qquad\qquad\qquad (3.2.5)$$

$$\frac{\partial \sum P_i}{\partial \lambda_{ik}} = F_{ik} = 0 \qquad \begin{aligned}(i &= 1, \ldots, R \\ k &= 1, \ldots, K)\end{aligned} \qquad (3.2.6)$$

The simplest way to prove that variable levels which meet these conditions also meet the Pareto efficiency conditions is to show that each of the conditions above is identical to its counterpart in section 3.1. We do not need to eliminate the Lagrange multipliers.

Equation (3.2.5) is identical to (3.1.9) (derivatives with respect to the externalities).

We can rewrite equation (3.2.3) for any two firms as

$$\lambda_{ik}\frac{\partial F_{ik}}{\partial v_{ikn}} = \lambda_{jk}\frac{\partial F_{jk}}{\partial v_{jkn}} \qquad \begin{aligned}(i, j &= 1, \ldots, R; i \neq j \\ k &= 1, \ldots, K \\ n &= 1, \ldots, N)\end{aligned} \qquad (3.2.7)$$

The same can be done for equation (3.1.7) so the first-order conditions involving ordinary inputs are identical.

Equations (3.2.4) and (3.1.8) can both be rewritten:

$$\sum_{k=1}^{K}\lambda_{ik}\frac{\partial F_{ik}}{\partial v_{ip}} = \sum_{k=1}^{K}\lambda_{jk}\frac{\partial F_{jk}}{\partial v_{jp}} \qquad \begin{aligned}(i, j &= 1, \ldots, R; i \neq j \\ p &= 1, \ldots, P)\end{aligned} \qquad (3.2.8)$$

so the first-order conditions involving joint inputs are identical.

We can rewrite equation (3.2.2) for any two firms as

$$\lambda_{i1}\frac{\partial F_{i1}}{\partial q_{il}} = \lambda_{j1}\frac{\partial F_{j1}}{\partial q_{jl}} \qquad \begin{matrix} (i, j = 1, \ldots, R; i \neq j \\ l = 1, \ldots, L) \end{matrix} \qquad (3.2.9)$$

so the first-order conditions involving saleable outputs are identical.

The production functions are identical so that part of the constraint equations in (3.2.6) and (3.1.10) is the same. The remaining constraints in the Pareto problem have their counterpart in the combined profit maximum problem if we simply write the definitions that total quantity of saleable output equals the sum of the amount produced by each firm and total quantity of ordinary and joint inputs equals the sum of the amounts purchased by each firm.

Since we have shown that the first-order conditions in the Pareto efficiency problem and the combined profit maximum problem can be manipulated until they are identical, we could derive conditions (3.1.12) and (3.1.14) from either set of first-order conditions. Again we note that (3.1.12) and (3.1.14) define an infinite number of efficient points. However, we know from convexity of the production function that there is a unique solution to equations (3.2.2) to (3.2.6) which maximizes combined profit, thus picking out one point on the locus of efficient points.

That one point has no special welfare properties beyond Pareto efficiency. It is just the point that will be reached if we start with a particular set of initial conditions. A particular set of output and input prices, given the production functions, determines a particular combined-profit-maximizing outcome. Different initial conditions will result in a different combined-profit-maximizing outcome, which will also be Pareto optimal.

We can justify intuitively the rule "maximize combined profit" in two ways. The first is to consider what happens if we merge the R firms and maximize profit *"as if" the merged firm were still a perfect competitor in all product and factor markets*. The fundamental theorem of welfare economics tells us that if firms acting as (by extension acting "as if") perfect competitors maximize their profit, the outcome is Pareto optimal so long as they impose no externalities on others. The unique set of outputs which maximizes the profit of the merged firm acting "as if" it is a perfect competitor is of course the same set of outputs that maximizes combined profit of the R firms. And, because all externalities produced or received by members of the group of R firms are received or produced only by others in the group, the "merged" firm has no externality relationship with others.

The second justification for the rule "maximize combined profit" is that it gives the greatest profit to be split up any way we wish among the R firms. Presumably this is desirable socially if all the firms in the economy are acting as perfect competitors. The other firms not in the set of R firms have their individual profit at a maximum by assumption and the R firms have the greatest amount of profit to divide among themselves. In this context we note the problem of distribution of profit among the R firms. When each firm is required to produce outputs which maximize combined profit, the outputs are Pareto optimal, but one firm (or several) may have profit less than it would have been had the firm maximized its profit in isolation. However, the profit distribution can be corrected by a lump sum transfer among firms which doesn't affect any firm's determination of its output level. Appendix (A.2) shows that a P.O. profit distribution (where no firm's profit can be increased without decreasing the profit of another firm) among R firms experiencing production externalities can be achieved only if outputs which maximize combined profit are selected.

The rule "maximize combined profit" is usually thought of as applying to the profit of the firms in their present line of business. However, Coase (1960) has shown that we must consider the profitability of alternative social arrangements. Often, closing down a firm and using its resources elsewhere will not always be more profitable socially than modifying its externality output,[11] but a general model must allow for both possibilities.

A properly constructed profit function will contain an item for fixed cost, which the economist would measure as opportunity cost of the resources owned by the firm.[12] Thus we can use the profit functions of the firms affected by externalities to compute the maximum social product of the firms in their present business versus that in the most attractive alternative. (At least, we can do this with theoretical profit functions. In the real world owned resources are not always valued "on the books" by their owners at opportunity cost, so it might be necessary to think up all the attractive alternative uses of the owned resources and compute their social products.) It is important always to remember, when considering externalities, that the decision whether to move a firm or use its resources

[11] This is particularly likely to be true when we use the generalized joint product model which allows for changes in method of production so as to get correct externality levels.

[12] That is, the value in the next best use of resources owned by the firm. We assume the raw materials and the resources hired by the firm to be obtained on a competitive market at opportunity cost.

in another line of business is not a marginal decision and cannot be made using marginal criteria. This limitation has not eliminated the use of marginal criteria in other fields, and it should not in the field of externalities.

It seems appropriate at this point to briefly summarize the major conclusions that have been drawn so far and chart the course of the rest of the work. A generalized joint production model has been presented which significantly generalizes the traditional treatment of production externalities. It was proved in section 3.1 that for efficient levels of externalities it is required that the marginal rates of technical substitution between a costly input and a public good externality summed over the firms receiving the externality equals the marginal social cost of producing the externality. It was then proved in section 3.2 that those externality levels which maximize combined profit of the firms affected by the externalities are efficient.

We note that simply computing Pareto optimal externality levels in no way modifies the behavior of the firms to make them choose these P.O. levels. Apart from having someone tell them that they must produce certain output levels, there are two major alternative approaches to the problem of giving firms incentive to do so—informationally centralized and decentralized approaches.

The rest of this book is divided into two major parts, corresponding in order to the centralized and decentralized approaches. The underlying rationale of informationally centralized solutions is that if we wish the firms to be guided by an invisible hand so that in maximizing their own profit they will choose P.O. outputs, *we may modify their profit functions by assigning proper "prices"*[13] *to these outputs.* The derivation of necessary and sufficient conditions for prices which insure P.O. outputs will be the subject of the next section.

3.3. Conditions for pricing schemes which enforce a stable Pareto optimum

This section will use the generalized joint product cost function introduced in section 2.2, model (2.2.6). Firm *i* then has the profit function (3.3.1) where initially we make no assumptions about its curvature or

---

[13] These "prices" correspond to Pigovian taxes/subsidies.

continuity:

$$P_i = pq_i' - k_i(q_i, X_i) \qquad\qquad (i = 1, \ldots, R) \qquad (3.3.1)$$

where p is a vector of prices and q_i is a vector of outputs of firm i. We assume that we have found the Pareto optimal outputs, q_i^*, X_i^* ($i = 1, \ldots,$ R) by maximizing combined profit as described in section 3.2. In general, the P.O. outputs differ from the vectors of outputs which maximize the equation (3.3.1), so we want to find "prices" (or charges) which enforce the socially optimal outputs.

It is not the purpose of this section to develop a specific pricing scheme. Here, we lay the groundwork for such a scheme by developing necessary and sufficient conditions which any such scheme must meet. It is better to do this abstractly than in the context of a particular scheme. We shall first develop completely general conditions which do not depend on assumptions of continuity or concavity of the profit function or on the techniques of marginalism. By extending these conditions to coalitions of firms, it will be possible to develop "prices" which, once assigned, are immune to criticism on game theoretic grounds. Then we shall use the general conditions to derive analogous conditions for the special case of concave profit functions. We shall more often work with the special conditions than the general ones, as the assumption of concave profit functions is usually considered defensible in price theory.

An optimal set of assigned "prices" must modify the profit functions of the firms so that the modified functions

$$E_i = pq_i' - k_i(q_i, X_i) + \phi_i(q_i, X_i)^{14} \qquad\qquad (3.3.2)$$

meet the following conditions:

> Each firm must find its individual profit at a maximum when it is producing the Pareto optimal level of each output under its control and all other variables affecting the firm are at P.O. levels. Therefore, the increase in profit of each firm from any increase (decrease) in any output under its control above (below) the P.O. level must be less than or equal to zero.

---

[14] The vectors of "price" functions, ϕ_i, are not assumed to be linear or continuous here. The important special case where the ϕ_i are linear functions is discussed in sections 4.1, 4.2, and 4.3. Also, price functions meeting the conditions of this section will be developed that do not assign prices to the saleable outputs, q_i. The q_i are included in the functional notation for generality.

67

Expressed in a convenient shorthand notation

$$\Delta E_i \text{ is } \leq 0 \text{ for any } \Delta x_{i0m} \text{ when } x_{i0m} = x^*_{i0m} \text{ }^{15} \qquad (3.3.3)$$

The increase in profit of each firm from any increase (decrease) in any output not under its control above (below) the P.O. level when all other variables affecting the firm are at P.O. levels must be less than or equal to zero.

$$\Delta E_j \text{ is } \leq 0 \text{ for any } \Delta x_{i0m} \text{ when } x_{i0m} = x^*_{i0m} \qquad (3.3.4)$$

Condition (3.3.3) is an obvious extension to generalized joint product pricing of the condition that is the (implicit) cornerstone of Pigovian taxes and subsidies. Condition (3.3.4), on the other hand, has not been suggested as a criterion for taxes and subsidies in previous work in the field of externalities and it will be shown in section 3.4 that the reason for the failure of standard Pigovian tax/subsidy schemes is that they do not meet this criterion.

I assert that, for profit-maximizing firms, conditions (3.3.3) and (3.3.4) are necessary and sufficient to guarantee that P.O. output levels are produced when firms are assigned prices meeting these conditions and allowed to maximize individually. Sufficiency is assured because the conditions mean that each firm wants to produce P.O. levels of all outputs under its control and wants every other firm to produce P.O. levels of all outputs that affect it.[16] As to the necessity: If condition (3.3.3) is not met, it is obvious that some firm will set outputs under its control at non-P.O. levels. If condition (3.3.4) is not met, firms will not want other firms to produce P.O. levels of externalities affecting them. The possible reactions will vary. In many cases, all that is needed to assure a stable Pareto optimum is a weaker version of these conditions (which appears in the next paragraph). However, we use the strict condition (3.3.4) because it is necessary when some firms have nonseparable cost functions and mutual externalities. In that situation, the profit-maximizing externality level of

[15] The notation $+\Delta P_i$ means an increase in the profit of i; Δx_{i0m} means any change, not necessarily marginal, in x_{i0m}. Outputs refer to nonsaleable joint outputs in this section because standard theorems of welfare economics prove that competitive prices ensure that P.O. levels of saleable outputs will be produced.

[16] The full demonstration of the sufficiency of these conditions in the special cases of nonseparable cost functions and non-convex cost functions will be made in sections 4.5 and 4.6.

firm i depends on the externality level of firm j. If (3.3.4) is violated, firms cannot be sure of getting the information necessary to set all their outputs at P.O. levels, and nonoptimal levels may exist temporarily or permanently. This will be explored in section 4.5.

When the profit-maximizing level of one firm's externality does not depend on another's level, (3.3.3) and a less strict version of (3.3.4) are sufficient to ensure optimality. If each firm wishes to set P.O. levels of externalities under its control and this doesn't affect other firms' output decisions, why should the others want to change the situation? The answer is that if (3.3.4) is violated, firm j would make a greater profit if i sets $x_{i0m} \neq x_{i0m}^*$. If j's gain in profit is less than i's loss from setting $x_{i0m} \neq x_{i0m}^*$, j alone cannot possibly conclude a bargain with i to deviate from the P.O. level.[17] However, j may still be able to join with a *group* of recipient firms to conclude a bargain with i to change x_{i0m} from the P.O. level. Thus we get the following condition that the profit functions of each firm modified by optimal assigned prices must meet:

The increase in the sum of profits of any combination of firms j ($j = 1, \ldots, R, \neq i$) from any increase (decrease) in output x_{i0m} of firm i above (below) the P.O. level when all other variables affecting the firms j are at P.O. levels must be less than or equal to the decrease in profit of firm i from that increase (decrease) in x_{i0m}[18,19]

$$\sum_j + \Delta E_j \leq -\Delta E_i \text{ for any } \Delta x_{i0m} \text{ when } x_{i0m} = x_{i0m}^* \qquad (3.3.5)$$

[17] One may wonder if there can actually be cases where j's gain in profit is greater than i's loss. Assessing charges which meet condition (3.3.3) but violate (3.3.4) will change the combined profit function such that in general there can be such cases. That is, if some level other than x_{im0}^* maximizes combined profit, a bargain (with side payment) is possible whereby both firms increase their profit by moving to that level.

[18] The terminology "any combination of firms j" means that we may sum the profits of any one firm, any two firms, $\ldots$, up to all r firms. There are $R - 1 + \binom{R-1}{2} + \cdots + \binom{R-1}{R-2} + 1$ such combinations.

[19] A consumption externalities version of this condition appears as equation (7), p. 354, of Buchanan and Stubblebine (1962). When this condition does not hold, a potentially relevant marginal externality, in the authors' terminology, is said to exist. Buchanan and Stubblebine were not concerned with finding price or tax/subsidy solutions to externalities problems, although it may seem obvious in retrospect that the converse of their equation (7) is a condition for optimal prices.

Condition (3.3.5) means that no coalition of firms can afford to pay firm i enough to induce i to produce more or less than the P.O. level of x_{i0m}. From (3.3.3) we know that firm i will have no incentive to produce any level other than x_{i0m}^* unless someone pays it to do so. Conditions (3.3.3) and (3.3.5) are necessary and sufficient for assigned prices which assure a stable Pareto optimum, except in the case of mutual nonseparable externalities, where (3.3.4) is necessary.

Condition (3.3.5) has some relevance to the discussion of "private bargains" as a solution to the externality problem. If a bargain among the firms can be reached which results in payments which modify the profit functions of the firms so as to meet (3.3.3) and (3.3.5), then the bargain need not specify any action other than making the payments. No output quotas and no mechanism to enforce anything other than the payments are needed. The really difficult problem, that of making the bargain, remains, and will be taken up in section 5.2.

Condition (3.3.4) has an analogous interpretation with respect to *cheating* by a firm after charges have been assigned. If (3.3.4) is not satisfied, it means that firm j wants firm i to produce some externality level other than the Pareto optimum. If firm j is unable to get i to produce the desired level through bargaining—either because (3.3.5) is met or because bargaining breaks down, it may resort to some form of trickery or cheating to accomplish its purpose. If (3.3.4) is satisfied, firm j has no incentive to get i to alter its P.O. output levels. This line of reasoning will play an important part in sections 4.5 and 5.1.

Conditions (3.3.3), (3.3.4), and (3.3.5) apply to firms with any kind of profit functions. They do not require continuity and concavity. These general conditions may be restated in a special form for the important case where we assume the modified profit functions, E_i, of (3.3.2) are strictly concave and possess continuous first partial derivatives. The partial derivatives of the E_i with respect to any of the variables will then unambiguously measure the increase in profit of firm i from a marginal change in the given variable, and a zero partial derivative will indicate a global maximum with respect to the variable. We can therefore restate the general conditions in terms of the derivatives.

An optimal set of assigned prices must modify strictly concave profit functions of the firms so that the modified functions meet the following conditions:

> The increase in profit of any firm from a marginal increase (decrease) in any output under its control above (below) the P.O. level must be zero.

(a) $\dfrac{\partial E_i(q_i^*, X_i^*)}{\partial q_{il}} = 0$
    $\qquad (i = 1, \ldots, R$
    $\qquad l = 1, \ldots, L)$

(b) $\dfrac{\partial E_i(q_i^*, X_i^*)}{\partial x_{i0m}} = 0$
    $\qquad (i = 1, \ldots, R$
    $\qquad m = 1, \ldots, M)$ \qquad (3.3.6)

Proof: It can be proved by contradiction that (3.3.3) implies this. From (3.3.3) the increase in profit of firm i from a marginal increase (decrease) in any output under its control above (below) P.O. levels must be less than or equal to zero. Now if a function is continuous and has continuous partial derivatives, then both right and left directional derivatives exist at any point and have the same magnitude but opposite signs. Therefore, if the increase in profit of i from an increase in its output is strictly less than zero, then the increase in profit of i from a decrease in its output must be strictly greater than zero and this contradicts (3.3.3). The continuity and differentiability assumption and (3.3.3) can hold simultaneously if and only if (3.3.6) holds.

> The increase in profit of any firm from a marginal increase (decrease) in any output not under its control above (below) the P.O. level must be zero.

$\dfrac{\partial E_i(q_i^*, X_i^*)}{\partial x_{j0m}} = 0$
$\qquad (i, j = 1, \ldots, R, i \neq j$
$\qquad m = 1, \ldots, M)$ \qquad (3.3.7)

Proof: The proof proceeds identically to that for (3.3.6). By the continuity and differentiability assumption, if the increase in profit of j from a marginal increase in i's output is strictly less than zero, then the increase in profit of j from a marginal decrease in i's output must be strictly greater than zero in contradiction to (3.3.4). Thus (3.3.7) must hold.

The increase in the sum of profits of any combination of firms j ($j = 1, \ldots, R, \neq i$) plus the increase in profit of firm i from a marginal increase (decrease) in output x_{i0m} above (below) the P.O. level must be zero.

$$\sum_j \frac{\partial E_j(q_j^*, X_j^*)}{\partial x_{i0m}} + \frac{\partial E_i(q_i^*, X_i^*)}{\partial x_{i0m}} = 0 \tag{3.3.8}$$

($i, j = 1, \ldots, R, i \neq j; m = 1, \ldots, M$) and for all possible combinations of subsets of firms j)

Proof: Again, the method of proof is identical to those above. We have from (3.3.6) that $-\Delta P_i = 0$. If the increase in $\sum_j + \Delta P_j$ from a marginal increase in x_{i0m} is strictly greater than zero, then by continuity and differentiability the increase in $\sum + \Delta P_j$ from a marginal decrease in x_{i0m} must be strictly less than zero. That, combined with zero $-\Delta P_i$, contradicts (3.3.5). To avoid contradiction, we must have $\sum_j + \Delta P_j = 0$, so (3.3.8) must hold.

In discussing the general conditions (3.3.4) and (3.3.5), we noted that the latter was weaker. We cannot say the same for (3.3.7) and (3.3.8). Given (3.3.6), (3.3.8) implies (3.3.7)[20] and vice versa.[21] Thus, we may use either condition for any concave profit function. Ockam's Razor would lead us to prefer the simpler (3.3.7) once we have gained from the other condition some insight into the bargaining process and the assurance that no weaker condition than (3.3.7) can be prescribed.

Thus, we hold that (3.3.6) and (3.3.7) are necessary and sufficient conditions that must be met by strictly concave modified profit functions if we are to achieve P.O. externality levels by a decentralized scheme of "price" incentives. Sections 4.1 and 4.2 will, respectively, show how to determine "prices" which so modify the profit functions, and prove that the conditions are met. The next section, 3.4, will examine some tax/subsidy schemes which have appeared in the literature and show why they violate our conditions.

---

[20] Consider the special case of (3.3.8) where the combination of firms j contains only one firm. Then because (3.3.6) makes the change in the profit of firm $i = 0$, the change in the profit of firm j must $= 0$, and we have condition (3.3.7).

[21] If $\partial E_j / \partial x_{i0m} = 0$ for each firm $j = 1, \ldots, R, \neq i$, then (3.3.8) must hold.

3.4. Demonstration that the "standard" Pigovian tax/subsidy schemes proposed to date fail to meet the conditions in section 3.3

In section 1.3, we examined the history of criticism of Pigovian tax/subsidy schemes. At the time Coase (1960) wrote, most economists seemed to agree that a tax based on damages caused or a subsidy based on benefits conferred would impel firms to produce P.O. outputs. Coase pointed out that the proponents of this solution did not direct that the tax be of a compensatory nature, that is, that it be paid to those damaged by the externalities.[22] Buchanan and Stubblebine (1962) and Turvey (1963) showed that if the tax is *not* paid to the injured firm, and if the firms are able to negotiate, a nonoptimal solution will result. One purpose of this section is to reconfirm this conclusion, first in a simple application of the "traditional" externalities model (1.3.1), and then for the generalized joint production model, expressed as a profit function, (3.3.1). We shall show that if a tax based on damages is not paid to the firm damaged, the profit function of the damaged firm, modified by any taxes that firm may be required to pay, does not meet condition (3.3.7) of the previous section.

Davis and Whinston (1962) carried the attack one step further, showing that if the externalities are nonseparable—that is, where profit of firm 1 is a nonseparable function of that firm's output and an output controlled by firm 2 [$P_1(q_1, q_2)$ cannot be written as $P_{11}(q_1) + P_{12}(q_2)$]—tax/subsidy schemes of the kind with which they were familiar will not work. Their use of game theory was unnecessary since the same conclusions can be gained without it. It is fairly clear that Davis and Whinston did not anticipate that the tax be paid to the firm damaged. If this is so, their conclusion is redundant, though interesting because it raises the issue of nonseparability. However, it can be shown, and that is the second purpose of this section, that even if a tax based on damages *is* paid to the firm damaged, when the profit function is nonseparable P.O. outputs will not be achieved. This eliminates taxes based on damages as a general solution to the externality problem.

[22] Or that the subsidy be collected from those benefited by external economies. We shall henceforth in this section make our argument in terms of diseconomies, but the arguments and conclusions for economies are precisely analogous.

In recent years, a different Pigovian approach has become popular. Under this approach, instead of being based on damage, a tax is computed whose purpose is to make each firm produce socially optimal levels of outputs under its control. Writers favoring or citing this approach also do not propose that the tax be paid to the firm damaged by the externality. The final purpose of this section is to show that, whatever the nature of the profit function, if the tax is not paid to the firm damaged, P.O. outputs will not be achieved.

This leads us to the almost obvious conclusion that a tax calculated to make each firm produce P.O. levels of outputs under its control will achieve its purpose if the tax is paid to the firm damaged. This conclusion, however obvious, has not been stated in the literature before. It must be proved to be true (which is quite a different matter from proving a statement false by counterexample) and this proof, along with some ramifications of the method, will occupy all of chapter 4.

SEPARABLE EXTERNALITIES, TAX BASED ON DAMAGE IS PAID TO CENTRAL AUTHORITY. Consider a general separable profit function model of the "traditional" type, model (1.3.1), where there are two firms, with firm 1 suffering from an external diseconomy directly related to the saleable output of firm 2:

$$P_1 = f_{11}(q_1) - f_{12}(q_2)$$
$$P_2 = f_2(q_2)$$

(3.4.1)

The combined profit of the two firms is given by

$$P = f_{11}(q_1) - f_{12}(q_2) + f_2(q_2)$$

(3.4.2)

and the P.O. outputs are those outputs q_1^* and q_2^* which satisfy the following first-derivative conditions (if we assume P is concave):

$$\frac{\partial P}{\partial q_1} = \frac{\partial f_{11}}{\partial q_1} = 0$$

(3.4.3)

$$\frac{\partial P}{\partial q_2} = -\frac{\partial f_{12}}{\partial q_2} + \frac{\partial f_2}{\partial q_2} = 0$$

(3.4.4)

Now the damage created by firm 2 is $f_{12}(q_2)$, so we make firm 2 pay that amount to the central authority. Firm 1 receives nothing. Thus its profit function, modified by taxes, has not changed.

$$E_1 = f_{11}(q_1) - f_{12}(q_2) \tag{3.4.5}$$

Outputs which maximize firm 1's profit are those which satisfy

$$\frac{\partial E_1}{\partial q_1} = \frac{\partial f_{11}}{\partial q_1} = 0 \tag{3.4.6}$$

$$\frac{\partial E_1}{\partial q_2} = -\frac{\partial f_{12}}{\partial q_2} = 0 \ ^{23} \tag{3.4.7}$$

Firm 2's profit function *does* change:

$$E_2 = f_2(q_2) - f_{12}(q_2) \tag{3.4.8}$$

Outputs maximizing firm 2's profit satisfy

$$\frac{\partial E_2}{\partial q_2} = \frac{\partial f_2}{\partial q_2} - \frac{\partial f_{12}}{\partial q_2} \tag{3.4.9}$$

Now equation (3.4.6) is identical to equation (3.4.3), and (3.4.9) is identical to (3.4.4), so we see that firm 1 will, after taxes, *initially* set $q_1 = q_1^*$ and firm 2 will set $q_2 = q_2^*$. However, (3.4.7) is *not* the same as (3.4.4) so firm 1 doesn't want $q_2 = q_2^*$. Although firm 1 cannot directly set q_2, it can offer to pay firm 2 to change the level of q_2. If q_2 is at the P.O. level, which satisfies (3.4.4), only a small payment should be needed to induce firm 2 to lower q_2 a bit, because at q_2^* the decrease in firm 2's profit from a marginal decrease in q_2 is zero. We can see why it should be possible to make a bargain reducing q_2 by looking at the new *post-tax* combined profit function. The outputs which maximize this function are those which would be achieved in an optimal bargain and are those toward which all bargains tend.

$$E = E_1 + E_2 = f_{11}(q_1) + f_2(q_2) - 2f_{12}(q_2) \tag{3.4.10}$$

Outputs maximizing E must satisfy

$$\frac{\partial E}{\partial q_1} = \frac{\partial f_{11}}{\partial q_1} = 0 \tag{3.4.11}$$

$$\frac{\partial E}{\partial q_2} = \frac{\partial f_2}{\partial q_2} - 2\frac{\partial f_{12}}{\partial q_2} = 0 \tag{3.4.12}$$

[23] The derivative of E_1^* with respect to q_2 doesn't aid firm 1 in setting its optimal output, except in the case where it can control q_2. We shall see in a few paragraphs how this derivative assumes importance.

The outputs satisfying (3.4.11) and (3.4.12) are those which would be achieved in an optimal bargain, and they are not the same as the P.O. outputs satisfying (3.4.3) and (3.4.4).

Only if the firms are *totally unable* to make a bargain will they settle for the P.O. outputs. It is not necessary to claim that an optimal bargain will always be reached. Any bargain will result in socially nonoptimal outputs being produced. It is not even necessary to prove that any bargain *must* be reached, only that it *can* be. (Thus there is no contradiction between the results here and my contention in section 5.2 that private bargains alone do not eliminate the need for some kind of collective action to achieve P.O. outputs. If we are to rely on private bargains alone to achieve P.O. outputs, it must be proved that optimal bargains are always achieved. That is not needed when the bargaining argument is used, as it is here, as a counterexample.)

Now that we have seen how this line of reasoning works in the simplest model, (1.3.1), we can generalize by applying the same taxation scheme to the generalized joint product model. We assume R firms have separable profit functions of the form of (3.3.1). The P.O. outputs are those which maximize combined profit of the R firms. It is the intent of the taxation system of the type we are considering to make firms damaging others pay a tax to a central authority. Thus the functional relationship expressing the effect of j's output on i's profit function is not changed by the imposition of this taxation system. The derivative of i's modified profit function with respect to j's output, $\partial E_i / \partial x_{j0m}$, remains the same as the pretax derivative, $\partial P / \partial x_{j0m}$, and its value will not generally be zero at the P.O. output levels.[24]

Condition (3.3.7) is therefore violated by this solution. Condition (3.3.6) (that the derivatives of the E_i with respect to the variables under i's control, evaluated at P.O. output levels, be zero) is met. Thus the firms will initially produce P.O. output levels, but it will be to their advantage to enter bargains which increase the profit of each firm but result in socially nonoptimal output levels.

SEPARABLE EXTERNALITIES, TAX BASED ON DAMAGE IS PAID TO FIRM SUFFERING DAMAGE. Model (3.4.1) again applies. This time firm

---

[24] In the case where x_{j0m} is an external diseconomy for firm i over its whole range, the derivative will usually be negative for $x_{j0m}^* > 0$. When x_{j0m} is an external economy over its whole range, we may expect the derivative to be positive for any finite x_{j0m}^*.

1 receives the tax and its modified profit function is

$$E_1 = f_{11}(q_1) - f_{12}(q_2) + f_{12}(q_2) \tag{3.4.5}'$$

As we see, the last two terms cancel and the sole first-derivative condition is (3.4.6). As this is the same as (3.4.3), the first-derivative condition for P.O. outputs, it is clear that firm 1 will produce the P.O. level of q_1 and will be indifferent as to the level of q_2. Firm 2's modified profit function is the same as (3.4.8) so it will produce q_2^* and be indifferent to the level of q_1. Since the combined modified profit function E is the same as P, the combined pre-tax profit function, we can see that there would be no profit in bargaining away from the P.O. output levels.

We will reach the same conclusion if this taxation scheme is applied to the generalized joint product model. Because the terms involving x_{j0m} are cancelled from i's modified profit function, the derivative of E_i with respect to x_{j0m} is zero at the P.O. output levels (as it is at all levels). Thus condition (3.3.7) is satisfied.

So far we have shown that, for separable externalities, a tax based on damage will not work if it is paid to the center, but will work if it is paid to the firm damaged. What may we conclude for nonseparable externalities? The work of Davis and Whinston (1962) unfortunately does not help us much, because they did not explicitly consider the case where a tax is paid to the damaged firm. Their work seems to consider only the case where the tax is paid to the center. Their conclusion, that with nonseparable externalities a tax/subsidy system will not work, could be deduced from the work of Buchanan and Stubblebine (1962) or the analysis of this section,[25] although they add a different and interesting argument. In the next few paragraphs, we shall extend their use of a nonseparable function explicitly to the case where a tax is paid to the damaged firm. However, we shall not use their game theoretic formulation, as that seems to be unnecessary.

By getting what are essentially nonsense results, we shall show that a tax based on damage will not enforce P.O. levels of mutual nonseparable externalities.

NONSEPARABLE EXTERNALITIES, TAX BASED ON DAMAGE IS PAID TO FIRM SUFFERING THE DAMAGE. Consider a version of model (1.3.1)

[25] That is, it is not nonseparability that vitiates a scheme where the tax is paid to the center; rather it is the bargaining away from a P.O. which will occur with *any* profit function.

with mutual nonseparable externalities:

$$P_1 = f_1(q_1, q_2)$$
$$P_2 = f_2(q_1, q_2)$$

(3.4.13)

Each firm is able to control only the level of its own output, but its output decision is affected by the level of the other firm's output.[26] The first-order conditions for a maximum of each firm's profit are

$$\frac{\partial P_1}{\partial q_1} = \frac{\partial f_1(q_1, q_2)}{\partial q_1} = 0$$

(3.4.14)

$$\frac{\partial P_2}{\partial q_2} = \frac{\partial f_2(q_1, q_2)}{\partial q_2} = 0$$

(3.4.15)

Since 1's output decision depends on 2's decision and vice versa, the initial output choices when each maximizes in ignorance of the other's choice (that is, when each solves its equation for the variable it can control using an *estimate* for the other variable) may be modified in successive rounds of an iterative process. The process is discussed in Davis and Whinston (1962) and Wellisz (1964) and in section 4.5 of this book, and need not concern us here. If the iterative process converges to a stable solution, the levels of the variables are given by the simultaneous solution of (3.4.14) and (3.4.15).

Combined profit of the two firms is given by

$$P = f_1(q_1, q_2) + f_2(q_1, q_2)$$

(3.4.16)

and the P.O. outputs, q_1^* and q_2^*, must satisfy the following first-order conditions, assuming P to be concave:

(a) $$\frac{\partial P}{\partial q_1} = \frac{\partial f_1(q_1, q_2)}{\partial q_1} + \frac{\partial f_2(q_1, q_2)}{\partial q_1} = 0$$

(b) $$\frac{\partial P}{\partial q_2} = \frac{\partial f_1(q_1, q_2)}{\partial q_2} + \frac{\partial f_2(q_1, q_2)}{\partial q_2} = 0$$

(3.4.17)

[26] Since we intend to show that nonseparability can result in non-P.O. externality levels if the tax is based on damage, we can use a simple model such as this. The proof is in the nature of a counterexample. The same result can be proved for a "broad" joint product model where the externality does not bear a one-to-one relationship with the saleable output.

78

As we can see, the P.O. outputs correspond to neither the initial nor the final solution values of (3.4.14) and (3.4.15).

How do we evaluate the prescription "each firm must compensate the other for the damages it suffers"? It would seem that "damage" should be the difference between the profit a firm would make if the externality affecting it were zero and the profit it would make if the other firm set the externality at whatever level it wished. Since that level is affected by imposition of the damage scheme, it is a variable. Thus we get the following damage payments:

$$1 \text{ pays } 2 \quad f_2(q_1 = 0, q_2^0) - f_2(q_1, q_2) = a_2 - f_2(q_1, q_2)$$

$$2 \text{ pays } 1 \quad f_1(q_1^0, q_2 = 0) - f_1(q_1, q_2) = a_1 - f_1(q_1, q_2)$$

The first term in each damage function is a constant because we can solve maximum P_i for some unique q_i^0 given $q_j = 0$.

Given these damages, the modified profit functions are

(a) $\quad E_1 = f_1(q_1, q_2) + a_1 - f_1(q_1, q_2) - a_2$

$\qquad + f_2(q_1, q_2)$

(b) $\quad E_2 = f_2(q_1, q_2) + a_2 - f_2(q_1, q_2) - a_1$

$\qquad + f_1(q_1, q_2)$ \hfill (3.4.18)

The first-order conditions for firm 1 to have profit at a maximum are

$$\frac{\partial E_1}{\partial q_1} = \frac{\partial f_1(q_1, q_2)}{\partial q_1} - \frac{\partial f_1(q_1, q_2)}{\partial q_1} + \frac{\partial f_2(q_1, q_2)}{\partial q_1} = 0 \qquad (3.4.19)$$

Firm 2's first-order conditions are

$$\frac{\partial E_2}{\partial q_2} = \frac{\partial f_2(q_1, q_2)}{\partial q_2} - \frac{\partial f_2(q_1, q_2)}{\partial q_2} + \frac{\partial f_1(q_1, q_2)}{\partial q_2} = 0 \qquad (3.4.20)$$

The first two terms in each first-order condition cancel, leaving us with only one term in each equation. 1 now sets q_1 so as to maximize P_2 and 2 sets q_2 so as to maximize P_1. This implies zero or infinite values of the outputs depending on whether the externality is a diseconomy or an economy. There is no tendency to iterate to a different solution because the level of q_i which maximizes P_j does not depend on q_j; thus, for example, firm 1 won't change its output as q_2 is altered; q_1 equal to zero or infinity always maximizes P_2.[27] These are the nonsense results promised earlier. This solution does not, in general, correspond with the P.O. solution.

Now, if we add E_1 and E_2, we will find that the combined after-tax profit function is the same as the before-tax combined profit function, P. Thus we know that there is incentive for the firms to enter a bargain whereby the P.O. outputs are produced. *However, it is not the imposition of a rule of compensation that gives them this incentive;* they had equal incentive before compensation was ordered. Nor is it certain, in spite of the incentive to agree to produce P.O. outputs, that they will do so; in fact it is quite doubtful, as is shown in section 5.2.

The conclusion reached in the preceding paragraphs, that ordering a tax based on damages to be paid to the damaged party will not necessarily bring about P.O. output levels if the externalities are nonseparable, has not been reached explicitly in previous work. However, it seems to have been implicitly recognized, since in recent years interest in taxation schemes based on damages (no matter to whom the damages are paid) has waned. Those who are still interested in centralized Pigovian tax/subsidy approaches seem to be discussing the type which will be considered in the next paragraphs.[28]

TAX WHOSE PURPOSE IS TO MAKE FIRMS PRODUCE P.O. LEVELS OF OUTPUTS UNDER THEIR CONTROL IS PAID TO CENTRAL AUTHORITY. With the one exception noted in footnote 28, those proposing or citing

---

[27] This statement must be qualified slightly: If q_1 is first an economy and then a diseconomy, for example, P_2 will be at a maximum at some particular value of q_1 between 0 and infinity. This value of q_1 may even vary with the level of q_2, but in any event, there is no reason to expect it to correspond with the P.O. value since that is not set to maximize P_2 but rather $P_1 + P_2$.

[28] Wellisz (1964) is one exception to this trend although not a proponent of damage schemes. Wellisz's method derives a *non-linear* tax/subsidy function for each firm which modifies the firm's profit function such that (a) each firm's profit is a function only of outputs under its control, (b) each firm, in maximizing its modified profit function, chooses outputs which maximize pre-tax combined profit, i.e., P.O. outputs. It was noted in section 1.3 that this scheme is in fact the first general proof that there does exist a determinate tax/subsidy scheme having the properties sought by Pigou (and satisfying the conditions of section 3.3 of this paper). The scheme proposed in section 4 should be considered as an alternative to Wellisz's method. The primary difference between the two methods is that the method in section 4 gives constant tax levels. It is therefore a shadow pricing method, and we can determine and prove a number of properties of such a price system.

Pigovian tax/subsidy approaches still direct that the tax be paid to a central authority and that the subsidy (to a firm producing an external economy) come from a central authority. Fairly specific methods for computing taxes and subsidies are specified in Henderson and Quandt (1958), Davis and Whinston (1962) and (1967), and McManus (1967).[29] All of these approaches give (constant)[30] taxes/subsidies which induce each firm to initially produce P.O. levels of those outputs under its control. Thus these schemes satisfy conditions (3.3.6) of the previous chapter. However, because the tax paid by firm j on its output is not given to firm i, the functional relationship expressing the effect of j's output on i's profit function is not changed by the imposition of the tax. Therefore, the derivatives $\partial E_i/\partial x_{j_0 m}$ remain the same as the pre-tax derivatives $\partial P_i/\partial x_{j_0 m}$ and their value will not generally be zero when evaluated at the P.O. output levels. These schemes therefore violate condition (3.3.7) of the previous chapter. The firms will initially produce P.O. output levels, but it will be to their advantage to enter bargains which increase the profit of each firm but result in non-P.O. output levels. This is, of course, the same conclusion we reached for taxes based on damage created.

We have demonstrated in this section that whether a tax is based on damages created or on forcing firms to produce P.O. levels of outputs under their control, and whether the externalities are separable or non-separable, if the tax is paid to the center instead of to the firm damaged it cannot guarantee that P.O. outputs actually will be produced. We have also shown that if the externalities are nonseparable, a tax based on damages will not work even if it *is* paid to the firm suffering the damage,

What conclusion are we to draw for the Pigovian approach? It might

---

[29] The latter two articles derive taxing schemes for consumption externalities. It may not be fair to suggest them for production externalities although any scheme which works for the former ought to work for the latter as a special case. We also note that Davis and Whinston, at least in their 1962 article, are attacking the scheme they present, although not for the reasons it is attacked here. Finally, it should be pointed out that all of these schemes were applied by their authors to the "traditional" model of externalities, (1.3.1). They are applied here to the generalized joint production model so we can use directly the notation of section 3.3. The traditional model is a special case of generalized joint production, so we would arrive at the same conclusion.

[30] These schemes give constant taxes because the taxes are found by evaluating a derivative at a single (optimal) point. The function giving revenue from taxes (tax times externality level) is therefore linear.

seem by analogy that a tax forcing firms to produce P.O. levels of outputs under their control will work if it is paid to the firm suffering the damage, with the possible exception of the nonseparable case. However, it is not a simple matter to prove this, as it was for the tax based on damages. Condition (3.3.7) tells us that we must prove that the taxation system which makes firm j produce x^*_{j0m} will also make firm i (with its different profit function) *want j* to produce x^*_{j0m}. Furthermore, we must deal with the question of nonseparability. For this reason, the next chapter will detail a precise algorithm of joint product pricing. For joint products that are externalities, this algorithm is a tax/subsidy scheme where the tax is paid to the firm damaged and the object is to make firms producing externalities want P.O. levels to be produced. It will be proved that the algorithm achieves this goal and that nonseparability offers no problem.

FOUR

GENERALIZED JOINT PRODUCT PRICING SCHEMES

4.1. Algorithm to determine externality charges

Earlier sections have suggested the hypothesis that for every external diseconomy a constant tax per unit can be found that will impel a profit-maximizing firm to produce a Pareto optimal level of the externality. It is further hypothesized that if this tax is divided up appropriately and paid to the firms receiving the diseconomy, they will want the P.O. amount of the externality to be produced. Then, by conditions (3.3.6) and (3.3.7), this tax will guarantee that the P.O. externality level is reached and maintained. The symmetrical hypothesis for an external economy is that an optimal subsidy to the producing firm, paid by the beneficiary firms, can be found. This section sets forth an algorithm for finding the hypothesized taxes or subsidies in an informationally centralized manner. A concluding subsection offers a straightforward graphical interpretation of the algorithm.

We begin, as usual, with the model of generalized joint production of section 2.2. We first find those output levels which maximize combined profit, the P.O. outputs. We then modify each firm's profit function by assigning a vector of unknown (constant) "prices." Finally, we form equations of the form of (3.3.6) and (3.3.7) (the conditions for optimal assigned prices), substitute the P.O. output levels, and thus find the optimal prices.

All the notation needed for this section and section 4.2 is given here. Repetition of some definitions is for convenience.

P_i = "profit" or net rent of firm i.

$k_i(q_i, X_i)$ is a strictly convex cost function for firm i ($i = 1, \ldots, R$).

$q_i = (q_{i1}, q_{i2}, \ldots, q_{il}, \ldots, q_{iL}); (i = 1, \ldots, R; l = 1, \ldots, L);$ a vector of outputs of firm i, where q_{il} is the output by i of product l.

$X = (x_{i0m}, x_{j0m})_{j,m}$ $(j = 1, \ldots, R, \neq i; m = 1, \ldots, M)$, an R by M matrix of externalities relevant to firm i. x_{i0m} is the amount produced by i and received by each other firm. x_{j0m} is produced by j.

$p = (p_1, p_2, \ldots, p_l, \ldots, p_L); (l = 1, \ldots, L)$, a vector of competitive market prices for the outputs q_{il}.

$C_i = (c_{i0m}, c_{jim})_{j,m}$ $(j = 1, \ldots, R, \neq i; m = 1, \ldots, M)$, an R by M matrix of externality charges, to be determined, each element corresponding to an element of X_i.

c_{i0m} is the total price received by i from all other firms for 1 unit of x_{i0m} produced by i. It is calculated from i's modified profit function as we shall see in (4.1.9). $-c_{jim}$ is the price paid by i to j for 1 unit of x_{j0m} as calculated from i's modified profit function. If x_{j0m} is an external diseconomy, $c_{jim} \geq 0$ (or $-c_{jim} \leq 0$).

$D_i = (c_{i0m}x_{i0m}, c_{jim}x_{j0m})_{j,m}$ $(j = 1, \ldots, R, \neq i; m = 1, \ldots, M)$, an R by M matrix in which each element is the product of an element in C_i and the corresponding element in X_i.

Firm i's profit is given by

$$P_i = pq'_i - k_i(q_i, X_i) \qquad (i = 1, \ldots, R) \qquad (4.1.1)$$

P.O. outputs are those outputs which maximize combined profit:

$$\sum_i P_i = p \sum_i q'_i - \sum_i k_i(q_i, X_i) \qquad (i = 1, \ldots, R) \qquad (4.1.2)$$

The necessary conditions for a maximum to (4.1.2) are given by

$$\frac{\partial \sum P_i}{\partial q_{il}} = p_l - \frac{\partial(\sum k_i(q_i, X_i))}{\partial q_{il}} = 0 \qquad \begin{matrix} (i = 1, \ldots, R \\ l = 1, \ldots, L) \end{matrix} \qquad (4.1.3)$$

$$\frac{\partial \sum P_i}{\partial x_{j0m}} = - \frac{\partial(\sum k_i(q_i, X_i))}{\partial x_{j0m}} = 0 \qquad \begin{matrix} (i, j = 1, \ldots, R \\ m = 1, \ldots, M) \end{matrix} \qquad (4.1.4)$$

By the assumption of convexity of the k_i, (4.1.2) has a unique maximum, the vectors q_i^* and matrices X_i^* $(i = 1, \ldots, R)$, which satisfy (4.1.3) and (4.1.4).[1]

---

[1] The sum of strictly convex functions is a strictly convex function and its negative is a strictly concave function which has a unique maximum. By assuming the k_i are convex, we avoid the "Baumol problem" in which the second-order conditions for a maximum of the social welfare function are violated. See Appendix D.

To find the matrices of unknown (constant) prices, C_i, we form the modified individual profit functions

$$E_i = pq_i' - k_i(q_i, X_i) + sD_it' \qquad (i = 1, \ldots, R) \qquad (4.1.5)$$

where s and t are sum vectors, $s,t = (1, 1, \ldots, 1)$, having as many elements as D_i has rows and columns respectively.[2]

The necessary conditions for a maximum to E_i are given by equations (4.1.6) and (4.1.7). These equations are of the same form as (3.3.6) and (3.3.7), the conditions for optimal assigned prices.

$$\frac{\partial E_i}{\partial q_i} = p - \frac{\partial k_i(q_i, X_i)}{\partial q_i} = 0 \qquad (i = 1, \ldots, R) \qquad (4.1.6)$$

$$\frac{\partial E_i}{\partial X_i} = -\frac{\partial k_i(q_i, X_i)}{\partial X_i} + C_i = 0 \qquad (i = 1, \ldots, R) \qquad (4.1.7)$$

We find C_i by evaluating (4.1.7) at the P.O. values q_i^*, X_i^* to get

$$C_i^* = \frac{\partial k_i(q_i^*, X_i^*)}{\partial X_i} \qquad (i = 1, \ldots, R) \qquad (4.1.8)$$

The notation in (4.1.8) was used to convey the point that, once optimal outputs are known, the matrix of charges relevant to firm i is found by using firm i's cost function, k_i, and P.O. values of only those variables relevant to firm i (its own saleable outputs and externalities affecting it). Let us now look at the elements of C_i^*:

$$\text{(a)} \quad c_{i0m}^* = \frac{\partial k_i(q_i^*, X_i^*)}{\partial x_{i0m}} \qquad (m = 1, \ldots, M)$$

$$\text{(b)} \quad c_{jim}^* = \frac{\partial k_i(q_i^*, X_i^*)}{\partial x_{j0m}} \qquad \begin{matrix} (j = 1, \ldots, R, \neq i \\ m = 1, \ldots, M) \end{matrix} \qquad (4.1.9)$$

Thus we see that both the "price" received by i for the externality it produces and the "price" paid by i for the externality it consumes must equal its marginal cost evaluated at P.O. variable levels for changes in the externality. This result is not surprising; when marginal revenue from any change in a variable equals marginal cost from that change, the firm cannot

---

[2] sD_it' becomes a scalar giving the sum of the elements in D_i:

$$\left(\sum_m c_{i0m}x_{i0m} + \sum_j \sum_m c_{ijm}x_{i0m} \right)$$

or the total receipts by i for the externalities it produces less the total payments by i for the externalities it receives.

increase its profit by the change and therefore doesn't want to see the change occur. A rigorous proof that this is so for the "optimal charge" algorithm will be given in section 4.2.

We haven't yet worked out the relation between c^*_{i0m}, the charge received by firm i for its externality, and $\sum_j c^*_{ijm}$, the combined charges paid by the recipient firms for that externality. Intuitively, we expect the two quantities to be the same but, since the "center" could absorb the difference, we shall examine this question among others in section 4.3.

GRAPHICAL EXPOSITION. The most compact and simple way to show how the "optimal charge" algorithm works is to diagram a two-firm example. The extension to several firms clutters up the figure and can be described better in a few words.

Assume first that firm 1 produces an external economy, x_{101}, which firm 2 "consumes." Firm 1's and firm 2's total cost curves with x_{101} varying and other variables fixed (hence the notation $\bar{q}_i$, $\bar{X}^o_i$) are shown in the upper and lower panels respectively of Figure 17. For fixed levels of the other variables, combined total cost is minimized where the distance between the two curves is smallest; or, equivalently, where their slopes are equal, that is, at the point x^*_{101}.[3] Now if all other variables are at their P.O. levels, it is clear that x^*_{101} maximizes combined profit.[4]

It was noted earlier that the optimal charge is equal to the marginal cost of each affected firm evaluated at P.O. variable levels for changes in the externality. Thus the line expressing revenue from the charge has the same slope as TC has at x^*_{101}. For the external economy producer, the revenue is positive. It is negative for the "consumer," who pays the subsidy. The same line will do for both if we treat the upper panel of Figure 17 as negative income for firm 2. Each firm will choose that level of x_{101} where the revenue minus the cost it generates is algebraically greatest. Firm 1 will produce, and firm 2 will want 1 to produce, x^*_{101}.

[3] If there are several recipient firms, we may add their cost curves vertically. Where the combined curve and TC_1 are closest minimizes combined cost.

[4] For nonseparable cost functions we get different combined cost-minimizing x_{101} levels for each set of values of the other variables. The multidimensional cost surfaces are closest together at different points in the x_{101} dimension depending on our position in the dimensions of the other variables. For separable functions, cost-minimizing x_{101} doesn't vary with the level of the other variables. In either case, at P.O. levels of all other variables, there is only one level of x_{101} which minimizes combined cost and therefore maximizes combined profit.

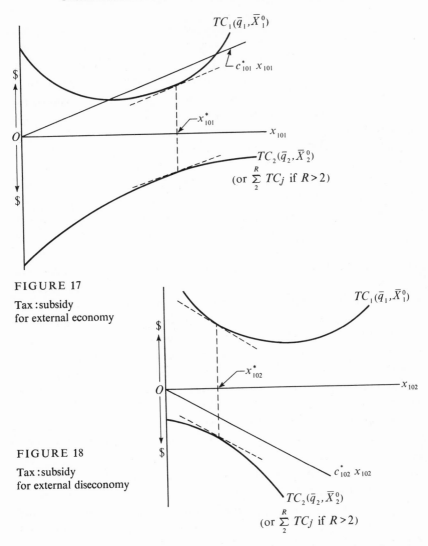

FIGURE 17

Tax : subsidy
for external economy

FIGURE 18

Tax : subsidy
for external diseconomy

If there are several recipient firms, we can represent the subsidy each pays by a total revenue line ($c^*_{1j1}x_{101}$) having the same slope as firm j's TC curve at x^*_{101}. The vertical sum of all these revenue lines must equal the revenue line of firm 1. This point will be proved rigorously in section 4.2, where it is shown that $c^*_{i0m} = -\sum_j c^*_{ijm}$. Each recipient firm will want x^*_{101} to be produced.

87

If firm 1's cost function is nonseparable with respect to its two outputs x_{101} and q_{11}, for example, revenue is represented as a plane surface with its origin at $q_{11} = 0$, $x_{101} = 0$ and rising in both directions from there. The TC function is a curved surface, convex from below, with $TC = 0$ at $q_{11} = 0$, curving upward along the q_{11} axis, and having sections as shown in Figure 17. The profit maximum is where the slopes of TC and TR are equal in both directions. This describes the simultaneous choice of both outputs. Figure 17 describes the choice of x_{101} when q_{11}^* has already been found. Since at q_{11}^* (if it is > 0) the revenue plane cuts the $\$$ axis above 0, $c_{101}^* x_{101}$ shown here is a line parallel to the revenue plane. It represents the portion of the revenue attributable to the externality.

Figure 18 depicts firm 1 producing an external diseconomy, x_{102}, which firm 2 "consumes." The producer's TC curve, shown in the upper panel, is similar in shape to that in Figure 17. The recipient's cost rises with the level of the diseconomy, so we should expect the combined profit-maximizing level to be less than that which is optimal for the producer acting alone. The optimal charge makes the diseconomy's contribution to total revenue negative for the producer and positive for the recipient, so the revenue line is in the lower panel of Figure 18. Again we see that a charge equal to marginal cost makes both firms want the externality level to be x_{102}^*.[5]

Now that we have drawn these figures, we can more easily explain the conventions we have adopted as to sign and direction of payment in defining the elements of the matrix of "prices." c_{101} is the "shadow price" received by firm 1 for an externality which it produces. It is positive if 1 is an external economy which we want to increase, because MC_1 (the slope of TC_1) is positive at x_{101}^*. Firm 1 receives a negative "payment" for its external diseconomy because MC_1 is negative at x_{102}^*. $-c_{121}$ is the "price" paid by 2 for the externality produced by 1. Since C_2 is a matrix of revenues, we write it as c_{121}. At any level (including the optimum) of the external economy x_{101}, MC_2 is negative, so, by (4.1.9), c_{121} is negative and

---

[5] Again, we are only depicting the part of each firm's decision that relates to choice of x_{102}. We are taking a two-dimensional slice of the multidimensional figure depicting both firms' simultaneous choice of all variable levels. If cost functions are separable, the choice of x_{102} is not affected by the choice of other variables; if they are nonseparable, the choice must be made simultaneously. In either case, when market prices are given for all saleable outputs and optimal charges are assigned for all externalities, the condition with respect to x_{102} which must be satisfied for optimal choice is shown in Figure 18.

$-c_{121}$ is positive. For an external diseconomy, x_{102}, MC_2 is positive, so $-c_{122}$ is negative. When there are only two firms, as in Figure 17 and 18, $-c_{121} = c_{101}$ so we can use the latter term to express both the charge paid and the charge received.

THE ISSUE OF CENTRALIZATION. The tax/subsidy scheme we have described in this section has the purpose of achieving P.O. production without eliminating the decentralized character of decisions in a market economy. Proponents of such schemes feel intuitively that a system is more efficient (or somehow more "free") if production is guided by corrective taxes rather than by output directives.[6]

The tax/subsidy scheme we have described in this section is decentralized in this decisional sense, but it is informationally centralized. That is, the "center" must know the cost functions of the firms in order first to calculate the P.O. variable levels and then to calculate the charges. It is clear that even with the honest cooperation of the firms involved, this is a severe requirement. And, unfortunately, welfare economics in its present state doesn't permit approximations.[7] Imperfect information gives imperfect results; and, like a stern religion, welfare economics condemns all degrees of imperfection equally.

Apart from the fact that firms don't know their cost functions perfectly (a regrettable imperfection that we might choose to dispense with in a theoretical discussion), the logical deduction is made that firms have an incentive to transmit incorrect cost functions to the "center" so as to mislead it into issuing more advantageous charges. There is no answer to this criticism in the uncompromising logic of welfare economics. If we could tolerate some imperfection, we could reduce the incorrect transmission of cost functions by random audits.[8]

[6] No claim should be made as to the relative robustness of corrective taxes versus output directives in the face of changing states of the world; static analysis as well as the second-best theorem permits no such comparison.

[7] Any of the current proposals for taxes on pollutants represents an approximation of this sort. None is made with complete information on the cost functions involved.

[8] There are also approximation approaches which don't require knowledge of the entire multidimensional cost function. For example, we could estimate marginal cost of changes in an externality level for producer and recipient in the neighborhood of the current variable levels, institute a modest tax or subsidy, allow some time for movement toward new equilibrium values of all variables, estimate marginal cost again, and so on, for a few iterations.

If informationally decentralized tax/subsidy schemes were significantly better, we should jump to their advocacy. However, as we shall see in section 5.1, the *tatonnement* scheme of Davis and Whinston shares a common disadvantage with centralized schemes and has one all its own. The "private bargain" solution (section 5.2) is similarly blessed. For the time being, we should study both informationally centralized and decentralized schemes without being advocates of either, as we can learn from both.

4.2. Theorems on externality "prices"

We shall prove three theorems of fairly self-evident significance. The first is that the algorithm we have just presented really meets the conditions of section 3.3. Next, we shall prove that the total price, c_{i0m}^*, received by firm i per unit of its production of externality m must equal the *sum* of the prices, c_{ijm}, paid by firms $j = 1, \ldots, R, \neq i$, per unit of the externality. It is important to note that the pricing algorithm (4.1.8) and the theorem proved here for externalities are general for all public production goods (for example, goods provided by the government as a "service to production") where the public goal is optimal production. We note that this theorem does *not* require that the same price be charged to each firm for the public production good, x_{i0m}. Finally, we shall show that the "price" should be the same for all producers of an identical externality.

> *Theorem 1: Externality prices, C_i^*, will cause the firms, maximizing individually, to prefer P.O. output levels.*[9]

Having been assigned the prices C_i^*, firm i's modified profit function is

$$E_i = pq_i' - k_i(q_i, X_i) + sD_i^*t' \qquad (i = 1, \ldots, R) \qquad (4.2.1)$$

where D_i^* is understood to mean the matrix where each element is the product of an element of C_i and the corresponding element of X_i.

---

[9] The most important elements of this proof were suggested by Enrique Arzac. His advice throughout most of Chapter 4 has been indispensable.

The necessary conditions for a maximum to (4.2.1) are

$$\frac{\partial E_i}{\partial q_i} = p - \frac{\partial k_i(q_i, X_i)}{\partial q_i} = 0 \qquad (i = 1, \ldots, R) \qquad (4.2.2)$$

$$\frac{\partial E_i}{\partial X_i} = -\frac{\partial k_i(q_i, X_i)}{\partial X_i} + C_i^* = 0 \qquad (i = 1, \ldots, R)^{10} \quad (4.2.3)$$

Substituting (4.1.8) for C_i^* in (4.2.3) and rearranging terms, we get

$$\frac{\partial k_i(q_i, X_i)}{\partial X_i} = \frac{\partial k_i(q_i^*, X_i^*)}{\partial X_i} \qquad (i = 1, \ldots, R) \qquad (4.2.4)$$

Equations (4.2.4) state, for each i, the equality of two vectors, and the corresponding elements of each vector must be equal. Thus we get equations of the form

$$\frac{\partial k_i(q_i, X_i)}{\partial x_{j0m}} = \frac{\partial k_i(q_i^*, X_i^*)}{\partial x_{j0m}} \qquad \begin{matrix} (i, j = 1, \ldots, R \\ m = 1, \ldots, M) \end{matrix} \qquad (4.2.5)$$

Now if the cost functions k_i are strictly convex, their first partial derivatives are monotonic. Since monotonic functions are one-to-one functions, we can make use of the definition: if a function F is one-to-one, then $F(x) = F(y)$ implies $x = y$.[11] Thus in (4.2.5) above, $q_i = q_i^*$ and $X_i = X_i$ for all i, j.

We noted earlier that because the k_i are strictly convex, $\sum P_i$ has a unique maximum, q_i^*, X_i^*. Convexity of the k_i also implies that the E_i have unique maxima, q_i, X_i, which, from the proof above, equal q_i^* and X_i^* respectively. Thus we are assured that *the C_i^* modify each firm's profit function in such a way that it will, by maximizing individually, choose unique externality output levels which are equal to the P.O. levels, and in addition will not want any firm to choose non-P.O. externality output levels.* The latter

---

[10] Firm i, in maximizing its profit, would normally take only the derivatives of (4.2.1) with respect to x_{i0m} $(m = 1, \ldots, M)$, the externalities under its control, accepting whichever values of the x_{j0m}, over j, m that are set by the other firms. In this proof, however, we take the derivatives with respect to all elements of X_i because we wish to prove that the prices C_i^* remove all conflict among the firms about output levels, i.e., we wish to find out what levels of the x_{j0m} firm i *wants*.

[11] Apostol (1957), Definition 2-7, p. 29. This definition can be applied in a very broad sense so x and y can be vectors. If x and y are vectors, $x = y \Rightarrow$ all elements in $x =$ the corresponding elements in y. Thus x is (q_i, X_i) and y is (q_i^*, X_i^*) and if $x = y$ then $q_i = q_i^*$ and $X_i = X_i^*$.

is because some of the elements of X_i^* are joint output levels of other firms than i. The proof just concluded shows that firm i, when assigned the prices C_i^*, will want these outputs, as well as its own, to be at P.O. levels.

> *Theorem 2: The total price received by firm i per unit of its production of an externality must equal the sum of the prices paid per unit by all the firms receiving the externality.*

$$c_{j0m}^* = - \sum_{i=1}^{R \neq j} c_{jim}$$

A different "price" for the externality x_{j0m} is computed using the cost function of each of the R firms. If the amount j expects to receive from all the other firms, $c_{j0m}^* x_{j0m}^*$, is to equal the sum of the payments each firm expects to make to j, $-\sum_i c_{jim}^* x_{j0m}^*$, then $c_{j0m}^* = -\sum_i c_{jim}^*$. But will the equality hold? We must prove it.

In (4.1.5) we saw that the P.O. value of x_{j0m}^* is that value at which

$$\frac{\partial \sum P_i}{\partial x_{j0m}} = - \frac{\partial (\sum k_i(q_i, X_i))}{\partial x_{j0m}}$$

$$= - \sum_i \frac{\partial k_i(q_i, X_i)}{\partial x_{j0m}} = 0 \qquad (i = 1, \ldots, R) \qquad (4.2.6)$$

Because x_{j0m} is an externality, treated as a public good, it appears in each firm's cost function and therefore all R of the possible derivatives appear in the expression on the right above. Thus the following must hold when the derivatives are evaluated at P.O. values of the relevant variables:

$$\frac{\partial k_j(q_j^*, X_j^*)}{\partial x_{j0m}} = - \sum_i \frac{\partial k_i(q_i^*, X_i^*)}{\partial x_{j0m}}$$

$$(i = 1, \ldots, R, \neq j) \qquad (4.2.7)$$

From (4.1.9) we know that

$$c_{j0m}^* = \frac{\partial k_j(q_j^*, X_j^*)}{\partial x_{j0m}} \qquad (4.2.8)$$

and

$$c_{jim}^* = \frac{\partial k_i(q_i^*, X_i^*)}{\partial x_{j0m}} \qquad (i = 1, \ldots, R, \neq j) \qquad (4.2.9)$$

92

Substituting (4.2.8) and (4.2.9) into (4.2.7) we get

$$c^*_{j0m} = - \sum_i c^*_{jim} \qquad (i = 1, \ldots, R, \neq j) \qquad (4.2.10)$$

We can see from (4.2.10) and (4.2.9) that there is no requirement that the price charged for externality x_{j0m} be equal for each of the firms $i = 1, \ldots R, \neq j$. In general, it will not be since each firm's marginal cost evaluated at P.O. variable levels may be different from each other firm's.

This theorem guarantees that a tax/subsidy scheme based on this algorithm is self-sufficient: the "center" need not expend its own resources except on administration. The theorem can be applied to public production goods (weather forecasting, rainmaking, some R&D, etc.), but it should not be permitted to mislead. If the entity producing a public good of this sort has a downward-sloping MC curve, this pricing scheme may lead to negative profit. The government may have to subsidize the activity or alter the pricing scheme so as to pass some of the recipient's surplus on to the producer.[12] The theorem does show that, for efficiency, a "benefit" scheme of pricing is required.[13]

> *Theorem 3: The "price" should be the same for all producers of an identical externality.*

$$c^*_{j0m} = c^*_{r0m}$$

This result may be shown, almost trivially, by defining "identical externalities" and applying the pricing algorithm. We can define two externalities of the same type produced by different firms (say, x_{j0m} and x_{r0m}) as identical if they have the same effect on the cost function of each of the $R - 2$ recipient firms.[14] This means that a firm's MC with respect to

---

[12] This contingency is much less likely when the good is an externality. An externality is always produced as a by-product. Given charges C^*_i, the firm's choice is between producing P.O. levels of all variables or shutting down the joint activity altogether. Seldom would an externality charge make the entire activity unprofitable.

[13] Of course it should be noted that the "price" we are discussing is not of the "take it or leave it" variety; the fact that we cannot generally exclude consumers of a public good requires that the price be in the nature of a tax.

[14] If x_{j0m} and x_{r0m} have the same effect on k_i, we must write the latter in the special form

$$k_i(q_i, X^o_i, x_{j0m} + x_{r0m})$$

This is necessary because the effect of increments of the externality on k_i generally varies with the externality level. This relation will play no part in the proof, however, and so is not incorporated explicitly in the notation above.

variations in x_{j0m} equals its MC with respect to x_{r0m} when both are evaluated at the same values of all variables. Then, specifically,

$$\frac{\partial k_i(q_i^*, X_i^*)}{\partial x_{j0m}} = \frac{\partial k_i(q_i^*, X_i^*)}{\partial x_{r0m}} \qquad (i = 1, \ldots, R, \neq j, r) \qquad (4.2.11)$$

Therefore

$$\sum_{i=1}^{R \neq j, r} \frac{\partial k_i(q_i^*, X_i^*)}{\partial x_{j0m}} = \sum_{i=1}^{R \neq j, r} \frac{\partial k_i(q_i^*, X_i^*)}{\partial x_{r0m}} \qquad (4.2.12)$$

Thus, from (4.1.9) and Theorem 2, we know that

$$c_{j0m}^* = c_{r0m}^*$$

Naturally, this theorem will not apply when increments of x_{j0m} and x_{r0m} do not have identical effects on each k_i. For example, if m is a type of smoke coming from two different plants at different distances from firm i, units of m measured at the different sources will not have the same effect on i's cost function. It is reasonable in this case that the unit tax received by i from the two producers of m should not be the same.[15]

4.3. Application of the generalized joint product pricing algorithm to the transfer price problem

In the theory of the divisionalized firm, a problem which bears striking similarity to the externality problem is the "transfer price" problem. When one division of a firm is an internal supplier and produces a product which it transfers to another division, it is necessary to assign a price to the transferred product so that the divisions involved have a decentralized initiative to maximize firm profit. It was shown by Cook (1955) that when the transferred product is also sold on an outside competitive market, the proper transfer price is the competitive price. However, frequently there is no competitive price for the transferred product. Hirshleifer (1956), in the most important contribution to the transfer price problem, found the optimal transfer price for the following very restrictive problem (which is

---

[15] If we adopt the notation discussed in footnote 8, chapter 2, the effect on k_i of an increment of m *measured at* i will be the same for both producers of m. The functions $c_{jim} = f_{jim}^{-1}(c_{jim})$ and $c_{rrm} = f_{rim}^{-1}(c_{rim})$ will convert c_{jim} and c_{rim} into different taxes measured at the source.

restated and formalized here):

$$P_1 = -k_1(q_1) + p^*q_1$$
$$P_2 = p_2q_2 - k_2(q_2) - p^*hq_2 \qquad (4.3.1)$$

where the subscripts refer to divisions, h is a constant of proportionality ($q_1 = hq_2$), and p^* is the transfer price. q_1 is the transferred product and q_2 is the final product.

The firm's profit is maximized when ($P_1 + P_2$) is maximized. Hirschleifer shows that the condition for maximization is that the sum of the marginal costs of the divisions equals the marginal revenue of the final product, or p_2. He says that the center (firm management) could of course tell the divisions what levels of q_1 and q_2 to produce. "It is simple, however, to devise a transfer price rule which will lead the divisions autonomously to the same solution."[16] The rule is to have Div. 1 give to Div. 2 a price schedule for q_1, showing how much 1 would sell 2 at any given price. If Div. 1 is told to engage in marginal cost pricing (i.e., to ignore its role as the only seller), the schedule will be identical to Div. 1's marginal cost at each level of q_1. Div. 2, if it doesn't act as a monopsonist, will, in effect, treat Div. 1's marginal cost (the transfer price schedule) as its own cost. Div. 2 will thus maximize its profit by equating marginal revenue of the final product with its marginal cost which is now the sum of the marginal cost of the two divisions. The outputs which maximize firm profit will be produced.

This scheme is completely decentralized except for the instructions from the firm for each division to act as a perfect competitor in its relations with the other division. Hirshleifer, of course, realized that the divisions have incentive to "cheat" on this scheme by acting as monopolists. He did not say, though it follows directly from his work, that a transfer price can be computed *by the center* and assigned to the divisions that will eliminate the possibility of monopolistic action on the part of the divisions. To compute this, the center must know the cost functions of the divisions. The center finds the optimal outputs by setting the sum of the marginal costs of the divisions equal to the marginal revenue of the final product. It then evaluates the marginal cost of division 1 at the optimal q_1^* and sets that as *the* transfer price. This single transfer price is equal to the point on Div.

---

[16] Hirshleifer (1956), p. 174.

1's transfer price schedule that would be finally arrived at when Div. 2 has chosen the optimal output levels under Hirshleifer's decentralized scheme. The centralized scheme would be preferable to simply ordering the divisions to produce certain outputs since it would give them profit incentive to produce the optimal outputs instead of just an order to do so. Monopolistic action by the divisions would not be possible, but of course the informational requirements would be greater than under the decentralized alternative.

Whether we adopt a centralized or decentralized version of Hirshleifer's work, we note certain problems. Although it is somewhat restrictive to assume that Div. 1 produces no other product than the transferred product, it is much more restrictive to assume that Div. 2 cannot vary the amount of the transferred product it uses per unit of its own production. It is even more restrictive to assume, as Hirshleifer was forced to, that there can be no externalities between the divisions. Thus, a more general approach to the transfer price problem seems to be needed.

At this point, I should mention two other important works on the transfer price problem that adopt the Hirshleifer model but do not generalize it in the direction I have suggested. Whinston (1962) formulated a mathematical programming version of the Hirshleifer transfer price model, (1.3.2), and determined prices in an informationally decentralized manner. Whinston's price-generating algorithm is related to the Davis-Whinston algorithm for externalities, and the comments on cheating of section 5.1 apply here as well. The work of Baumol and Fabian (1964) is primarily a contribution to the theory of mathematical programming, developing the notion of provisional dual prices which can be determined to correspond to any feasible (but not necessarily optimal) solution of a primal problem. However, they show that when a multidivisional firm is represented by a mathematical program (that is, when we assume that there are constrained, or owned, resources), it may not be possible to determine a single transfer price which can induce the divisions to produce the (company) optimal solution. This is true most importantly because optimal solutions are not necessarily on the boundary of a division's feasible region since a company constraint may make feasible for the company only a subregion of a division's feasible region. While their result does not apply directly to the transfer price model introduced in this book, it is an important limitation on extensions of that model.

96

All of these restrictions can be eliminated by using the form of the generalized joint product cost function and making some small changes in definitions and notation. Thus the profit function of division i of an R-division competitive firm is

$$P_i = pq_i - k_i(q_i, X_i) \qquad (i = 1, \ldots, R) \qquad (4.3.2)$$

where q_i is a vector of saleable outputs of the division and p is a price vector as before. The only new notation is in the elements of X_i:

$X_i = (x_{ijm}, x_{jim}, x_{i0m}, x_{j0m})_{j,m}$ $(j = 1, \ldots, R, \neq i; m = 1, \ldots, M)$, a $(3R - 2)$ by M matrix of joint products relevant to Div. i.

Private good—x_{ijm} is the level of good m produced by i and received by j. x_{jim} is produced by j and received by i. $x_{i \cdot m} = \sum_j x_{ijm}$

Public good—x_{i0m} is the amount produced by i and received by every other division. x_{j0m} is produced by j.

$$\{x_{i0m}\}_i = \{x_{i0m}\}_1 = \{x_{i0m}\}_2 = \cdots = \{x_{i0m}\}_R$$

(The numbers to the right of the brackets represent the division measuring the output.)

The usual formulation of the transfer price problem implicitly assumes that products transferred among divisions are private goods: the consumption of one division reduces the amount available for others. These goods may be produced, as we usually assume, by diverting inputs from some other use; or they may be by-products. Both methods of production are consistent with the private good notation we have used.

Externalities are also transferred among divisions. We formulate them as public goods in (4.3.1), and the same notation can also apply to public goods of the Bowen-Lindahl-Samuelson variety which are transferred among divisions. Thus the formulation above generalizes the transfer price problem as to the conditions of production of the intermediate product and as to its use by the recipient division (which can now treat it as it does any input without using it in fixed proportion to output).[17]

What links externalities and transferred products is that they are outputs of a production entity for which there are no market prices to guide allocation. This connection suggested the use of a single model to cover

[17] Many of the elements in X_i will always be missing. Good m will be *either* a private or a public good. It also may not be produced by all firms.

them both. And the fact that all externalities and many transferred products are produced along with some other output of the entity suggested the use of a joint product formulation.

Transfer prices (and charges on interdivisional externalities) can be found by using the algorithm of section 4.1. Only the definition of the elements in C_i^* needs to be changed.

> $C_i^* = (c_{ijm}, c_{jim}, c_{i0m}, c_{jim})_{j,m}$, a $(3R - 2)$ by M matrix, each element corresponding to an element of X_i. c_{ijm} is the price received by i from j for 1 unit of x_{ijm}. $-c_{jim}$ is the price paid by i to j per unit of x_{jim}. c_{i0m} and $-c_{jim}$ are public good prices and are defined as in section 4.1.

TRANSFER PRICE THEOREMS. The three theorems on externality "prices" of the previous section will naturally apply to the "prices" we calculate for externalities and public goods transferred among divisions of a firm. However, our description of a transfer pricing mechanism for private goods is not complete until we explore the properties of that mechanism. We shall prove four theorems (numbering them 4 to 7 for continuity) which constitute a description of the transfer pricing mechanism and a demonstration that it achieves its objectives. The first shows that transfer prices computed using algorithm (4.1.8) cause divisions, maximizing individually, to prefer levels of transferred products which maximize firm profit. The next two show, respectively, that the transfer price is the same when computed using the producer's and the recipient's cost functions and when computed using the cost functions of two producers of the same product. One of the few significant theoretical contributions to the transfer price problem is the demonstration by Cook (1955) and Hirshleifer (1956) that the transfer price must equal the market price if the transferred product is also sold on a competitive market. This is proved rigorously here for the more general transfer price model of sections 4.1 and 4.2. It is proved at the same time that if an intermediate product of the private good variety is transferred to several divisions, the transfer price to each division must be the same.

> *Theorem 4: Transfer prices, C_j^*, will cause the divisions, maximizing individually, to prefer levels of transferred products which maximize firm profit.*

98

We need only sketch the outlines of a proof identical to that used for Theorem 1. When we assign prices according to the rule (4.1.8) and maximize the modified profit functions, we shall get first-order conditions of the form

$$\frac{\partial k_i(q_i, X_i)}{\partial x_{ijm}} = \frac{\partial k_i(q_i^*, X_i^*)}{\partial x_{ijm}}$$

$$\frac{\partial k_i(q_i, X_i)}{\partial x_{jim}} = \frac{\partial k_i(q_i^*, X_i^*)}{\partial x_{jim}} \qquad \begin{array}{l} (i, j = 1, \ldots, R; i \neq j \\ m = 1, \ldots, M) \end{array} \qquad (4.3.3)$$

By convexity of the k_i, these are monotonic and therefore one-to-one functions. $F(x) = F(y)$ implies $x = y$, so in (4.3.3) we have the desired result, that $q_i = q_i^*$ and $X_i = X_i^*$ for all i.

We know from (4.1.8) that a given (private good) transfer price, c_{ijm}^*, can be computed once using division i's and again using division j's cost function. If j's payment to i is to equal i's receipt from j, the price must be the same, whether computed using i's or j's cost function. But will they be the same? We can conceive of the "center" absorbing the profit or loss from a payments disequilibrium so if the prices are to be the same we must prove it. We introduce the notation

$$\{c_{ijm}^*\}_i = \text{optimal price computed using } i\text{'s cost function.}$$

Theorem 5: The transfer price on x_{ijm} computed using the producing firm's cost function must equal that computed using the recipient firm's cost function.

$$\{c_{ijm}^*\}_i = \{c_{ijm}^*\}_j$$

For firm profit (combined profit of the divisions) to be at a maximum, the first-order condition involving x_{ijm} is

$$\frac{\partial \sum P_i}{\partial x_{ijm}} = -\frac{\partial(\sum k_i(q_i, X_i))}{\partial x_{ijm}} = -\frac{\partial k_1(q_1, X_1)}{\partial x_{ijm}}$$

$$+ \frac{\partial k_2(q_2, X_2)}{\partial x_{ijm}} + \cdots + \frac{\partial k_R(q_R, X_R)}{\partial x_{ijm}} = 0 \qquad (4.3.4)$$

Now since x_{ijm} appears only in the cost functions k_i and k_j, only 2 of the R possible derivatives actually appear in the right-hand expression of (4.3.4) above. The following must therefore hold when the derivatives are evaluated at optimal values of the relevant variables:

$$\frac{\partial k_i(q_i^*, X_i^*)}{\partial x_{ijm}} = -\frac{\partial k_j(q_j^*, X_j^*)}{\partial x_{ijm}} \,^{18} \tag{4.3.5}$$

From (4.1.8) we know that

$$\{c_{ijm}^*\}_i = \frac{\partial k_i(q_i^*, X_i^*)}{\partial x_{ijm}} \tag{4.3.6}$$

and

$$\{c_{ijm}^*\}_j = \frac{\partial k_j(q_j^*, X_j^*)}{\partial x_{ijm}} \tag{4.3.7}$$

Substituting (4.3.6) and (4.3.7) into (4.3.5) we get

$$\{c_{ijm}^*\}_i = \{c_{ijm}^*\}_j \tag{4.3.8}$$

The foregoing is fundamentally a proof that the transfer pricing algorithm really defines a price system, that is, a system with the property that a single price will clear the market. Theorem 4 proves that the transfer price $\{c_{ijm}^*\}_i$ and $\{c_{ijm}^*\}_j$ will equate supply and demand for x_{ijm}, and Theorem 5 proves that these prices must be the same.

> *Theorem 6: The transfer price should be the same for all divisions producing a given transferred product.*

$$c_{jim}^* = c_{rim}^*$$

If good m is produced by two divisions, an increment of m must have the same effect on k_i whether it comes from division j or from division r. Thus:

$$\frac{\partial k_i(q_i^*, X_i^*)}{\partial x_{jim}} = \frac{\partial k_i(q_i^*, X_i^*)}{\partial x_{rim}} \tag{4.3.9}$$

Therefore, by (4.1.8), $\{c_{jim}^*\}_i = \{c_{rim}^*\}_i$ and, from Theorem 5, $\{c_{jim}^*\}_j = \{c_{rim}^*\}_r$.

As the final step in describing the properties of our transfer pricing mechanism, we prove a result that is quite important for the practical implementation of a transfer pricing scheme and bears on the so-called "make or buy" decision of managerial economics.

---

[18] Since (4.3.4) is among the necessary conditions for optimal values q_i^*, X_i^* ($i = 1, \ldots, R$), it must hold when evaluated at those values.

Theorem 7: The transfer price charged by one division for a given product must be the same for every division to which it supplies the product and must equal the competitive market price (if there is one) for that product.

We assume saleable product l to be the same as joint product m. The outputs in question are $q_{il}, x_{i1m}, x_{i2m}, \ldots, x_{iRm}$, the first being the saleable output of the given product, and the others being the amounts of the product transferred to other divisions by division i (there is no product x_{iim} or price c_{iim}^*). Since we are dealing with amounts of the same product disposed in different directions, we must express the cost function of firm i as a function of the sum of these amounts.[19] Thus:

$$P_i = p° q_i^{°\prime} + p_l q_{il}$$
$$- k_i[q_i^°, X_i^°, (q_{il} + x_{i1m} + \cdots + x_{iRm})] \qquad (4.3.10)$$

where we define $q_i^°$ to exclude q_{il} and $X_i^°$ to exclude the $x_{i1m}, \ldots, x_{iRm}$.

We assume that we have found optimal prices $c_{i1m}^*, c_{i2m}^*, \ldots, c_{iRm}^*$ and $C_i^{°*}$ (defined to exclude $c_{i1m}^*, \ldots, c_{iRm}^*$) which meet conditions (3.3.6) and (3.3.7). Therefore to maximize the modified profit function

$$E_i = p° q_i^{°\prime} + p_l q_{il} - k_i[q_i^{°*}, X_i^{°*}, (q_{il} + x_{i1m} + \cdots + x_{iRm})]$$
$$+ s D_i^{°*} t' + c_{i1m}^* x_{i1m} + \cdots + c_{iRm}^* x_{iRm} \qquad (4.3.11)$$

firm i must set the following derivatives equal to zero:

$$\frac{\partial E_i}{\partial q_{il}} = p_l - \frac{\partial k_i}{\partial q_{il}} = 0 \qquad (4.3.12)$$

$$\frac{\partial E_i}{\partial x_{i1m}} = c_{i1m}^* - \frac{\partial k_i}{\partial x_{i1m}} = 0 \qquad (4.3.13)$$

$$\vdots$$

$$\frac{\partial E_i}{\partial x_{iRm}} = c_{iRm}^* - \frac{\partial k_i}{\partial x_{iRm}} = 0 \qquad (4.3.14)$$

[19] We must express the cost function as a sum of the amounts of the product dispersed in different directions to account for the scale effect, if any. If unit cost is related to the number of items produced, it would be incorrect to treat the cost function otherwise. Constant returns to scale is included as a special case.

Using the chain rule, we can write the derivatives[20]

$$\frac{\partial k_i}{\partial q_{il}} = \frac{\partial k_i}{\partial(q_{il} + x_{i1m} + \cdots + x_{iRm})} \cdot \frac{\partial(q_{il} + x_{i1m} + \cdots + x_{iRm})}{\partial q_{il}}$$

$$= \frac{\partial k_i}{\partial(q_{il} + x_{i1m} + \cdots + x_{iRm})} \tag{4.3.15}$$

$$\frac{\partial k_i}{\partial x_{i1m}} = \frac{\partial k_i}{\partial(q_{il} + x_{i1m} + \cdots + x_{iRm})} \cdot \frac{\partial(q_{il} + x_{i1m} + \cdots + x_{iRm}}{\partial x_{i1m}}$$

$$= \frac{\partial k_i}{\partial(q_{il} + x_{i1m} + \cdots + x_{iRm})} \tag{4.3.16}$$

$$\frac{\partial k_i}{\partial x_{iRm}} = \frac{\partial k_i}{\partial(q_{il} + x_{i1m} + \cdots + x_{iRm})} \cdot \frac{\partial(q_{il} + x_{i1m} + \cdots + x_{iRm})^{[21]}}{\partial x_{iRm}} \quad .$$

$$\begin{array}{c} . \\ . \end{array}$$

$$= \frac{\partial k_i}{\partial(q_{il} + x_{i1m} + \cdots + x_{iRm})} \tag{4.3.17}$$

Since quantities which are equal to the same quantity are equal to each other, the derivatives in (4.3.15)–(4.3.17) are equal:

$$\left[\frac{\partial k_i}{q_{il}} = \frac{\partial k_i}{\partial x_{i1m}} = \frac{\partial k_i}{\partial x_{irm}} \right], \quad \text{so we can write:}$$

$$p_i = c^*_{i1m} = c^*_{i2m} = \cdots = c^*_{iRm} \tag{4.3.18}$$

Here is a case where we can directly observe the behavior of firms to see whether they follow the advice contained in this theorem.[22] It is a fair guess that many do not, setting the transfer price below the market price. Whether deviation from our advice can be justified if the transferred product is sold on imperfectly competitive markets and if so, under what circumstances, remains to be seen.

[20] Enrique Arzac suggested this step of the proof.

[21] The expression to the right of the multiplication sign in each of these equations is equal to 1.

[22] Note that we do not have to know anything about the cost function of any division to set the correct transfer price if the product is available on a competitive market.

4.4. Public and private good duality of generalized joint products

In section 3.1, it was shown that the conditions for efficient levels of generalized joint products, equations (3.1.11) and (3.1.13), could be interpreted analogously to Samuelson's optimality conditions for public consumption goods. Samuelson also noted

a remarkable duality property of public and private goods . . . Private goods whose totals add—such as $X_1 = X_1^1 + X_1^2$—lead ultimately to marginal conditions of simultaneous equality—such as $MC = MRS^1 = MRS^2$. Public goods whose totals satisfy a condition of simultaneous equality—such as $X_2 = X_2^1 = X_2^2$—lead ultimately to marginal conditions that add—such as $MC = MRS^1 + MRS^2$.[23]

It follows of course that the duality Samuelson noted for public and private consumption goods also holds for public and private production goods. Equation (3.1.11) may be interpreted as additive marginal conditions— $MC = MRS^1 + MRS^2$. Private production goods (including products transferred within a firm) are known to require marginal conditions of simultaneous equality.

The theorems proved in sections 4.2 and 4.3 may be consolidated and interpreted as a proof of quantity-price duality between public and private production goods. This is an extension of the kind of duality discussed in the previous paragraph. For the generalized joint product pricing model of section 4.1, we have proved in sections 4.2 and 4.3 the following duality relationships:

TRANSFERRED PRODUCTS—PRIVATE GOODS

$$x_{i \cdot m} = \sum_j x_{ijm} \qquad\qquad (j = 1, \ldots, R, \neq i)$$

$$\{c_{ijm}^*\}_i = \{c_{ijm}^*\}_j = c_{i1m}^*$$

$$= c_{i2m}^* = \cdots$$

$$= c_{iRm}^* \qquad\qquad (j = 1, \ldots, R, \neq i) \qquad \text{(Th. 5, 7)}$$

[23] Samuelson (1955). note 5, p. 353.

103

EXTERNALITIES—PUBLIC GOODS

$$\{x_{i0m}\}_i = \{x_{i0m}\}_j \qquad\qquad (j = 1, \ldots, R, \neq i)$$

$$c_{i0m}^* = -\sum_j c_{jim}^* \qquad\qquad (j = 1, \ldots, R, \neq i) \qquad \text{(Th. 2)}$$

(The $\cdot$ in the position of j signifies that $x_{i \cdot m}$ is the amount of the transferred product produced by i and transferred to all the other firms. The notation $\{\ \ \}_i$ means as computed in i's profit function.)

Thus, we see that, for private generalized joint products, whose quantities add, optimal prices must be simultaneously equal; while for public generalized joint products, whose quantities are equal, optimal prices are additive. The generalized joint product model applies to public and private goods which have no market in the usual sense. Of course competitive market prices for ordinary private goods must also obey the rules given in Theorems 5, 6, and 7.

The primary significance of the results we have proved here and in sections 4.2 and 4.3 lies not so much in the concept of duality as in the price relations themselves. Duality (or, more precisely, symmetry) is logically beautiful but means little more than that firm i's receipts from the "sale" of its generalized joint product must equal the payments by all other firms for that product whether the product is a public or a private production good.[24]

This section brings to a close the presentation of the generalized joint product pricing algorithm, the proof that it meets the conditions of section 3.3, and the development of its theoretical implications. We are left with several questions that have been raised by previous work in the field of externalities. The question of whether the algorithm works when a firm's cost function is nonseparable is treated in the next section, 4.5. The results there, although written from the point of view of externalities, apply as well to transfer prices. Appendices C and D then consider various sources of non-concave profit (or non-convex cost) functions and their implications for the pricing algorithm. These two sections apply only to externalities; no such problems arise with transferred products.

[24] We cannot automatically extend this result to public and private consumption goods and no attempt is made here to do so.

104

4.5. Nonseparable cost functions

When a firm's cost function (and therefore its profit function) is non-separable, the levels of its own outputs which maximize its individual profit depend on the level of the externality set by another firm. Thus, it must estimate the level of the other firm's externality before setting its own outputs. This section shows that, if certain convergence conditions are satisfied, the optimal externality "prices" C_i^* derived from equation (4.1.8) will modify the firm's profit function so that its estimate of the other firm's externality level and its own output levels will eventually converge on the P.O. levels after an iterative process. The primary conclusion of the section, however, is that such an iterative process is not necessary. Rather, it is argued, the fact that the prices C_i^* satisfy conditions (3.3.6) and (3.3.7) implies that each firm has all the information necessary to predict the externality level the other firm will set and that the prediction will be self-fulfilling. With optimal "prices," only rationality and the knowledge of rationality are required to bring about P.O. outputs. On a first reading, one may wish to skim the discussion of iterative processes so as to confront this conclusion sooner, as it is diametrically opposed to the often-quoted conclusion of Davis and Whinston (1962).

It was noted at the end of section 3.2 that we must consider at all times whether any kind of trickery or cheating is profitable for any firm, and it was shown in section 3.3 that if (3.3.7) is satisfied no firm has incentive to trick any other firm into producing non-P.O. output levels. This analysis will find an important use here, and it will be proved that with optimal "prices" not only will firms have the information and incentive to produce P.O. output levels but also no kind of cheating by one firm to get another to produce non-P.O. levels will pay. Furthermore, it will be shown that non-P.O. levels can be achieved only *temporarily* as the result of *unsuccessful* blackmail. Successful blackmail will result in P.O. outputs.

The analysis in this section will proceed in terms of the simplest possible model, a two-firm case of the traditional externalities model, equation (1.3.1). We assume each firm confers on the other firm an externality whose level is directly proportional to the "donor" firm's saleable output. Each firm's cost function is assumed to be nonseparable.[25] The

---

[25] The function $k_1(q_1, q_2)$ is separable if $k_1(q_1, q_2) = k_{11}(q_1) + k_{12}(q_2)$. The cost function is from model (1.3.1).

fundamental conclusion of this section, that the generalized joint product prices derived in section 4.1 will impel firms with nonseparable cost functions to cooperate benignly to produce P.O. outputs, holds quite generally for convex cost functions. The discussion of iterative processes can be generalized although it is not clear that any further insight would be gained.[26]

Davis and Whinston (1962) claimed that no tax/subsidy scheme would work because of the uncertainty inherent when one firm's decision rule

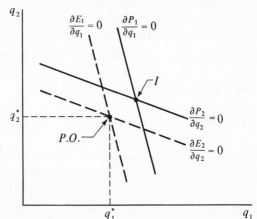

FIGURE 19

"Reaction curves" and "equilibrium" in a two-firm mutual nonseparable externality model. Source: Adapted from Wellisz (1964), Figure 1, p. 358.

includes as a variable the other firm's output. Sure enough, when optimal externality "prices" are assigned by the method described in section 4.1, firm i, given these "prices," may very well select an initial after "prices" profit-maximizing output, $\bar{\bar{q}}_i \neq q_i^*$. Let us examine a two-firm case where the cost function happens to be quadratic. In Figure 19, firm 1's "reaction curve" or decision rule *before* optimal "prices" is given by the solid line, $\partial P_1/\partial q_1 = 0$; its reaction curve after C_i is given by the dashed line, $\partial E_1/\partial q_1 = 0$. Similarly for firm 2. Whether or not prices C_i^* are assigned, firm 1 has to consider, in setting its output, the effect of firm 2's output level on its profit. Consider the situation without C_i^* assigned. Since firm 1 must take the world as it is and not engage in wishful thinking, it should

[26] The convergence proof, equations (4.5.1) through (4.5.9), cannot be very significantly generalized. It is only an illustration, however, of the point that there are some cost functions for which convergence does not occur; it is therefore in the nature of a counterexample, which does not need to be generalized to achieve its purpose.

estimate q_2 and set its q_1 accordingly. Firm 2 will do the same (estimate q_1 and set q_2, using $\dfrac{\partial P_2}{\partial q_2} = 0$), *and then firm 1 will revise its estimate* in the light of what firm 2 actually produced (or firm 1's estimate of what 2 actually produced). Point I is a possible equilibrium point which the firms might reach by maximizing individually and uncooperatively without central assistance in the form of externality "prices." (I is not the only possible point; bargaining and game theoretic considerations might result in a point somewhere between I and P.O.)

After optimal externality "prices" are assigned, the firms' decision rules are modified as shown by the dashed lines. If firm 1 estimates firm 2's output to be $\neq q_2$, $\bar{\bar{q}}_1$ will $\neq q_1^*$. However, firm 1 will revise its estimate of q_2 in succeeding iterations, and (this is the key point) because both firm 1 and firm 2 want $q_2 = q_2^*$ and both want $q_1 = q_1^*$, firm 1's estimate of q_2 will converge on q_2^* and therefore $\bar{\bar{q}}_1$ will converge on q_1^* (if certain conditions as to the stability of the equilibrium are met).

DERIVATION OF CONVERGENCE CONDITIONS. So far, we have not examined the method by which firm i estimates firm j's production at each iteration. Firm i may estimate firm j's production at iteration t as equal to what j produced at iteration $(t - 1)$. Or it may use any of a number of naive forecast models. For example, firm i may forecast that firm j will always move in the same direction in period t as it did in period $(t - 1)$ but at a slower rate. This will result in the following forecast: $\Delta q_2(t) = \delta \Delta q_2(t - 1)$, $0 < \delta < 1$. Or the direction of change may be negative.

In the case of two firms, each with a quadratic cost function, where firm i estimates firm j's production at iteration t as equal to what j produced at iteration $(t - 1)$, we can quite easily derive the conditions under which the iterative process will converge to a stable equilibrium. First we specify the profit functions

$$
\begin{aligned}
E_1 &= a_1 q_1^2 + b_1 q_1 + c_1 + d_1 q_1 q_2 + e_1 q_2^2 \\
&\quad + f_1 q_2 - c_1^* q_1 + c_2^* q_2 \\
E_2 &= a_2 q_2^2 + b_2 q_2 + c_2 + d_2 q_2 q_1 + e_2 q_1^2 \\
&\quad + f_2 q_1 + c_1^* q_1 - c_2^* q_2
\end{aligned}
\tag{4.5.1}
$$

where c_1 and c_2 are fixed costs, not "prices" like c_1^* and c_2^*.

Having found q_i^*, c_i^*, we can write each firm's decision rule as follows:

$$\frac{\partial E_1}{\partial q_1} = 2a_1 q_1 + b_1 + d_1 q_2 - c_1^* = 0$$

$$\frac{\partial E_2}{\partial q_2} = 2a_2 q_2 + b_2 + d_2 q_1 - c_2^* = 0$$ (4.5.2)

We will define the equilibrium production of firm i as Q_i, given by the simultaneous solution of equations (4.5.2). (Note that this also gives the P.O. values when c_i^* are used, as they are in [4.5.2]. Thus the equilibrium values are the Pareto optima. A rigorous proof of this would proceed as a special case of the proof of Theorem 1 in section 4.2.) The equilibrium value of q_1 is

$$Q_1 = -\frac{b_1 + d_1 Q_2 - c_1^*}{2a_1} = -\frac{b_2 + 2a_2 Q_2 - c_2^*}{d_2}$$ (4.5.3)

Let us replace (4.5.3) with a simpler equivalent expression:

$$Q_1 = A + aQ_2 = B + bQ_2,$$ (4.5.4)

where

$$A = \frac{c_1^* - b_1}{2a_1}, \qquad a = -\frac{d_1}{2a_1}$$

$$B = \frac{c_2^* - b_2}{d_2}, \qquad b = -\frac{2a_2}{d_2}$$

The dynamic model of this process is

$$q_1(t) = A + aq_2(t - 1) = B + bq_2(t + 1)$$ (4.5.5)

We arrive at (4.5.5) by making equations (4.5.2) dynamic: in $\partial E_1/\partial q_1$ expressing $q_1(t)$ as a function of $q_2(t - 1)$,[27] and in $\partial E_2/\partial q_2$ expressing $q_2(t)$ as a function of $q_1(t - 1)$; or, what is equivalent, expressing $q_1(t)$ as an inverse function of $q_2(t + 1)$. The explanation of this latter step is as follows: From (4.5.2) we have

$$q_2(t) = \frac{b_2 - c_2^* + d_2 q_1(t - 1)}{2a_2}$$

[27] This embodies the forecast model: firm 1 uses $q_2(t - 1)$ as an estimate of $q_2(t)$ in deciding on $q_1(t)$.

The inverse function (q_1 in terms of q_2) is

$$q_1(t-1) = \frac{b_2 - c_2^* + 2a_2 q_2(t)}{d_2}$$

One period later the function is

$$q_1(t) = \frac{b_2 - c_2^* + 2a_2 q_2(t+1)}{d_2} = B + bq_2(t+1)$$

At equilibrium, the dynamic model becomes

$$Q_1(t) = A + aQ_2(t) = B + bQ_2(t) \tag{4.5.6}$$

We subtract (4.5.6) from (4.5.5) to find the deviation from the equilibrium values

$$\Delta q_1(t) = a\Delta q_2(t-1) = b\Delta q_2(t+1) \tag{4.5.7}$$

The difference equation in t becomes

$$\frac{a}{b}\Delta q_2(t-1) = \Delta q_2(t+1) \tag{4.5.8}$$

or equivalently,

$$\Delta q_2(t) = \frac{a}{b}\Delta q_2(t-2)$$

The solution is

$$\Delta q_2(t) = (a/b)^{t/2}\,\Delta q_2(0) \tag{4.5.9}$$

Thus, if $b > a$, the deviation from equilibrium, $\Delta q_2(t)$, or $[q_2(t) - Q_2]$, decreases toward 0 as t increases without bound.

To complete the derivation of the convergence conditions we write the equivalent expressions to (4.5.5) and (4.5.6) for the production of firm 2. We get the same result, that $b > a$ assures convergence. Stated in terms of the original problem, our result is that $-2a_2/d_2 > -d_1/2a_1$ assures convergence.

What happens when this condition is not met (for example, when the slope of line $\partial E_1/\partial q_1 = 0$ is less than the slope of $\partial E_2/\partial q_2 = 0$ in Figure 11)?[28] More fundamentally, why should the firms go through the long,

---

[28] We can describe the iterative process graphically; it is similar to the "cobweb" process in demand-supply equilibrium.

costly (since profits are less than optimal until equilibrium is reached) iterative process described in these pages? There is no reason why they should!

There is an easier way for P.O. outputs to come about. Assume that the firms know that optimal prices have been assigned, meeting conditions (3.3.6) and (3.3.7). Firm j can use *its own* modified profit function to make a precise estimate of the level of x_{i0m} firm i will set. j knows i wants to set $x_{i0m} = x^*_{i0m}$ and j can find x^*_{i0m} simply by setting $\partial E_j / \partial x_{i0m} = 0$ and solving. Before optimal prices were given, no firm could predict the behavior of the other. So long as each firm knows the other is acting rationally, the circle of indeterminacy is broken. This will only be true when "prices" are assigned meeting conditions (3.3.6) and (3.3.7).

Neither firm can cheat on this process profitably because there is no conflict of interest between them. Their conflict of interest is resolved when (and only when) optimal charges are assessed. With any other set of charges (or none) firm 1's profit would be larger at some $q_2 \neq q^*_2$ and it would have incentive to somehow trick firm 2 into producing that non-optimal level. It would also adjust its own production accordingly, away from the Pareto optimum.[29]

Trickery will not really pay given optimal price matrices C^*_i and C^*_j. Say firm i wants to trick firm j—now j wants i to set $x_{i0m} = x^*_{i0m}$ because given C^*_j, any $x_{i0m} \neq x^*_{i0m}$ will result in less than optimal profit for firm j. Of course i can say to j, "You must pay me to set x_{i0m} at x^*_{i0m}, the level optimal for you." However, j can safely refuse, saying, "Go ahead. Set $x_{i0m} \neq x_{i0m}$. You will only lose by so doing." We remember that firm i's profit is also maximized at x_{i0m} given the optimal charges, C^*_i.

Even if i succeeds in blackmailing j, this only changes the profit distribution, not the output levels, if the blackmail payment is in lump sum form.[30] When i finally produces $x_{i0m} = x^*_{i0m}$ after j's blackmail payment, both firms' P.O. outputs, q^*_i, X^*_i and q^*_j, X^*_j, will be achieved. Thus we

[29] Actually, firm i knows that it can force j to produce x^*_{j0m} if j wants to maximize its profit. All i has to do is maximize its own profit by choosing outputs q^*_i, X^*_i, which includes x^*_{j0m}. (i knows that the level it wants of x^*_{j0m} is P.O. and is also the level j wants.) Once i produces output levels q^*_i, X^*_{ai}, firm j will have to produce x^*_{j0m} to maximize its own profit. *This is not true unless optimal prices are assigned.*

[30] Putting the payment in *non*-lump-sum form would cause the firms to end up producing non-P.O. levels. However, it would also reduce the profit the blackmailing firm could extort (because P.O. levels maximize combined profit) *so* the lump sum form *will* be chosen by a rational blackmailer.

arrive at this fundamental point: Because of the optimal assigned prices neither i nor j wants any other variable levels than the P.O. levels. Other levels will only be achieved temporarily as the result of *unsuccessful* blackmail (being forced to carry out a threat). If blackmail *works*, we will get P.O. outputs as we will in the absence of blackmail.

Optimal charges give the firms information they can use to produce exactly those levels of output which will make the blackmailer regret his bluff. Furthermore, when cooperation is not necessary for each firm to set P.O. output levels, attempted blackmail can be effectively banned by law.

FIVE

Decentralized Approaches
to the Externality Problem

This chapter discusses critically the two most important ways of handling the externality problem in a decentralized manner. The Davis-Whinston method is informationally decentralized, but with a central authority acting in a manner analogous to the Walrasian auctioneer. The private bargain approach is completely decentralized, with no government intervention whatsoever. Neither approach has received much fundamental criticism.[1] Since a decentralized approach, if it is workable, would be preferred by most economists, any weaknesses in these approaches should be brought out. In doing this, I do not wish to seem to be completely negative toward the concept of a decentralized way to compute externality taxes/subsidies. This concept deserves a great deal more study. The centralized method also has significant defects, to which others have given more attention than I have. While it may seem that I have devoted a great deal of space to centralized schemes, the theorems on externality "prices" (and transfer prices too) apply whether one computes them in a centralized or decentralized manner. So too does the demonstration that optimal "prices" work in the presence of nonseparable externalities.

5.1. The Davis-Whinston tax/subsidy algorithm

In a recent article, Davis and Whinston (1966) proposed an informationally decentralized, iterative scheme for determining optimal charges for the two-firm equivalent of (1.3.1), the traditional statement of the externality

---

[1] An article by Wellisz (1964) concerning, among other things, the private bargain approach, is the only fundamental criticism of either approach I have seen.

expressing the 7 Routhian conditions in terms of the original coefficients of the general quadratic problem would take *many* pages of text and the result would be meaningless in terms of placing useful restrictions on the original coefficients. Thus it is necessary to find the characteristic roots for specific quadratic problems, or to adopt the method of simulation of specific problems.

As simulation offers quite a bit more information than the method of finding characteristic roots, it was used here.[7] From the results of 40 computer runs, it can be seen that the Davis-Whinston algorithm does not always converge to stable equilibria which are Pareto optimal, and when it does converge, it often takes many periods to do so. For the problems run in this study, convergence and speed of convergence were quite sensitive to the values chosen for the adjustment coefficient, $\alpha_i(k)$. As that coefficient rose, up to a certain level for each problem, convergence speed rose; above that level it declined; as a certain critical level of $\alpha_i(k)$ was reached, divergence began. Convergence and speed of convergence were also sensitive to values chosen for the coefficients of the profit functions of the firms. For these 40 runs it was assumed that none of the output values could be negative, a realistic assumption not specified in the Davis-Whinston article. Another 40 runs were made with identical coefficient values but without restrictions on the output values. Here the tendency to diverge was much greater.

Davis and Whinston consider the problem of cheating only in the very limited context of a firm misstating its own output, and imply that a ready means exists for detecting such cheating.[8] They argue that should firm i cheat by understating its own output, this would reduce the charge on firm i but would also give it too low an output and would penalize firm j, presumably giving it incentive to protest. *I contend that firm i can also cheat by misstating x_j.* This means of cheating will not require it to propose nonoptimal $q_i(k)$—misstating x_j will not hurt firm i because x_j is really irrelevant to determining optimal $q_i(k)$; what is needed is $q_j(k)$[9]—nor will it

[7] Enrique Arzac helped write the simulation program.

[8] Davis and Whinston (1966), p. 317.

[9] x_j, as we remember, is the output of firm j *desired* by firm i; q_j is the output firm j *actually* produces. Firm i needs to know j's actual production in order to optimize his own when there are nonseparable externalities. When the externalities are separable, the level of q_j does not affect the optimal level of q_i. In any case, x_j is irrelevant to determining q_i. Thus, misstating x_j will *not* make it necessary for i to propose suboptimal q_i.

115

be detectable by the central authority or by firm j. Of course firm i's action will impose a penalty on firm j, but the latter will not know whether a given charge, $\lambda_j(k)$, comes as a result of a "fair play" or a cheating solution because it does not know firm i's profit function.

Let us examine a typical problem to see whether the type of cheating proposed here (misstating x_j, what one firm tells the authority it desires the other firm to produce) is advantageous to the cheating firm. As an example, I have chosen a case of mutual separable diseconomies where the cost function of each firm exhibits decreasing returns to scale in the relevant range and there is perfect competition on factor and product markets:

$$p_1 = 8$$
$$p_2 = 10$$
$$k_1 = 3q_1^2 - 5q_1 + 8 + 0.5q_2^2 + q_2 \tag{5.1.6}$$
$$k_2 = 4q_2^2 - 7q_2 + 11 + 0.2q_1^2$$

Both "fair play" and cheating solutions are summarized for a number of time periods in Table 1 on the next page. If the firms play according to the rules, at the end of the second time period (iteration 1) the values are: $q_1 = 1.98$, $x_2 = 0.06$; $q_2 = 1.99$, $x_1 = 2.71$.

Look at what has happened to x_1. At iteration 0, x_1 was 0.0, because firm 1's production brought only extra costs to firm 2. Given the charges for iteration 1, however, firm 2 would like firm 1 to produce 2.71 because then its gain from the charge (1.80 times 2.71) less its loss from the externality (0.2 times $[2.71]^2$) would be the greatest. *However, firm 1 is not going to produce 2.71 just because firm 2 wants it to; and herein lies the flaw in the Davis-Whinston argument.* For, on the next iteration, firm 2's high $x_1(1)$ is going to result in a smaller charge $\lambda_1(2)$ on firm 1 than it would have if firm 2 had understated $x_1(1)$. *Each time firm 2 understates x_1 it raises the charge on firm 1* (one of firm 2's prime sources of income) above what it would have been had firm 2 not cheated. This is one side of the coin. The other side is that if firm 2, by cheating, can raise $\lambda_1(2)$ over what it would have been in a "fair play" solution for iteration 2, firm 1, if it is playing fair, will come up with a smaller $q_1(2)$ than it would have otherwise.[10]

---

[10] The reason is that the coefficient of the q_1 term in firm 1's profit function, $[13 - \lambda_1(2)] q_1$, will be smaller, so the value of q_1 which makes the derivative $\dfrac{\partial P_1}{\partial q_1} = 0$ will be smaller.

TABLE 1. Davis-Whinston Algorithm for Separable External Diseconomies, Eqs. (5.1.6)

Iteration	q_1	q_2	x_1	x_2	λ_1	λ_2	P_1	P_2	P
"Fair play"									
0	2.17	2.12	0.00	0.00	—	—	1.70	6.12	7.82
1	1.99	1.99	2.71	0.06	1.08	1.06	1.97	6.24	8.21
2	2.05	1.87	1.81	1.03	0.72	2.03	4.73	3.65	8.38
3	2.03	1.82	2.11	1.45	0.84	2.45	5.23	3.12	8.42
4	2.03	1.80	2.01	1.63	0.80	2.63	5.72	2.70	8.42
5	2.03	1.79	2.04	1.72	0.82	2.72	5.84	2.59	8.42
6	2.03	1.78	2.03	1.75	0.81	2.75	5.91	2.51	8.42
7	2.03	1.78	2.03	1.77	0.81	2.77	5.94	2.49	8.42
8	2.03	1.78	2.03	1.77	0.81	2.77	5.95	2.48	8.42
9	2.03	1.78	2.03	1.77	0.81	2.77	5.95	2.47	8.42
10	2.03	1.78	2.03	1.78	0.81	2.78	5.96	2.47	8.42

Externality "price" solution given by (4.1.8)

	2.03	1.78	—	—	0.81	2.78	5.96	2.47	8.42

Combined maximum (centralized)

	2.03	1.78	—	—	—	—	2.67	5.76	8.42

Cheating by firm 2									
0	2.17	2.12	0.00	0.00	—	—	1.70	6.12	7.82
1	1.99	1.99	0.54	0.06	1.08	1.06	1.97	6.24	8.21
2	1.87	1.87	0.90	1.03	1.80	2.03	2.62	5.66	8.28
3	1.79	1.82	1.33	1.45	2.28	2.45	3.44	4.82	8.26
4	1.75	1.80	1.61	1.63	2.51	2.63	2.31	5.87	8.18
5	1.73	1.79	1.68	1.72	2.58	2.72	2.54	5.62	8.16
6	1.73	1.78	1.70	1.75	2.60	2.75	2.54	5.60	8.14
7	1.73	1.78	1.72	1.77	2.62	2.77	2.54	5.60	8.14

By reducing $q_1(2)$, firm 2 reduces its gain from the charge on firm 1, but it also reduces its loss from the external diseconomy caused by firm 1. The first effect of understating x_1—that of raising the charge on firm 1—far outweighs all other effects until q_1 gets very small. When q_1 gets small, the payment from firm 1 to firm 2 starts decreasing. Thus at some point, to protect its profits, the cheating firm must raise x_1 above 0 to prevent q_1 from going to zero.

Furthermore, firm 2 has to avoid being detected by the "center." It would be well advised to keep q_1 and P_1 from becoming too small. (Just how small is too small, we can't say. There is no *a priori* reason to expect q_1 and P_1 to move in any particular direction; suspicion-arousing values are a matter of judgment.) It can do this by keeping x_1 below its "fair play" level, but raising it steadily to promote convergence. And the charge, $\lambda_1(k)$, provides firm 2 with just the information it needs to bring about convergence. Since the *change* in λ_1 at each iteration is determined by the difference between q_1 and x_1, firm 2 can know whether to raise or lower x_1.[11]

We shall assume that firm 2 acts conservatively, raising x_1 from iteration 1 on, by this simple rule:

$$x_1(k) = x_1(k-1) + \beta[\lambda_1(k) - \lambda_1(k-1)]$$

It will change β frequently to avoid creating a pattern which will lead to detection. Starting with iteration 1 we use the following values for β: 0.5, 0.5, 0.9, 1.2, 1.0, 0.8, 0.9.[12]

Looking at the bottom section of Table 1, we can see the results of firm 2's strategy of cheating. λ_1 is forced steadily upward instead of downward, as in the "fair play" solution. Thus firm 2 is able to retain most of the profit it had before the "center's" intervention. By iteration 7, the algorithm is clearly converging on values approximately equal to $q_1 = 1.73$ and $q_2 = 1.78$. The difference between q_1 and x_1 and between q_2 and x_2 is getting very small, the "center's" signal that convergence is occurring. The cheater has done nothing to incur anyone's suspicion and has gotten away with profit of 3.13 above his "fair play" profit.

Firm 1 has no way of knowing that its profit should be above 2.54. One firm often has its profit reduced in a "fair play" of the Davis-Whinston algorithm (e.g., firm 2 in the top half of Table 1).

The "center" cannot detect cheating by looking at combined profit even though P appears to increase monotonically under "fair play" and not under cheating. First of all, the center may not give out each firm's output to the other firm at each iteration (this would be necessary for the firms to calculate their profit). If it did so, cheating would be facilitated because firm 2 would know $q_1(k)$ precisely—or at worst, know $q_1(k-1)$—

---

[11] But not how much to raise or lower it. Only the center knows α_i, the proportion of $(q_1 - x_1)$ by which λ_1 is increased.

[12] In practice, a less simple-minded rule would likely be used.

and could adjust x_1 better. Even if the "center" does publish the outputs, each firm's knowledge of its profit function is imprecise enough so that there could be honest error of the same order as the difference between P under cheating and under "fair play." In any event, firm 2 could adopt a more conservative strategy and practically assure monotonic increases in P.

Not all of the statements made with respect to separable externalities apply to the nonseparable variety. Because of the greater interdependence (extending now to the derivatives), *all* the variables of both firms are affected by firm 2's cheating. However, the same general conclusion holds for nonseparable external diseconomies: Firm i can successfully follow a policy of understating $x_j(k)$ for a while to raise the charge $\lambda_j(k + 1)$. Then to avoid detection and to keep firm j from closing down, firm i can gradually raise $x_j(k)$ toward $q_j(k)$, using the change in λ_j to indicate whether x_j should be raised, and retain or increase the profits it already has. This is true regardless of whether the authority truncates the iterative process before it has completely converged or not. This cheating is not without risks, but the risks are not of detection. Unless there is an elaborate spy system or frequent audits of nearly all firms, neither the aggrieved firm nor the authority can detect cheating. Measures such as audit of most firms (except audit on request of an aggrieved party) are not consistent with decentralization. If we are going to conduct such audits as would be necessary to keep cheating on the Davis-Whinston scheme within acceptable bounds, we might as well have the firms submit their profit functions to the authority and compute the charges centrally.

Thus we must conclude that the decentralized tax/subsidy scheme proposed by Davis and Whinston fails on two counts: first, either firm can cheat on the process, with the object of retaining or increasing its profit, by misstating to the center the level it desires of the other firm's externality; and second, even if the firms act honestly, the iterative process may not converge on the socially optimal charges and output levels.

In spite of these significant defects, the Davis-Whinston *tatonnement* scheme retains considerable promise. If the number of firms affected by each firm's externality is large, the prospects for success are a little better. A single firm would be unable to influence the level of the charges by misstating x_j; however, a coalition could influence the level of the charges.

It would be fairly difficult to get such a coalition to work, so the scheme might be successful. Further study may yield refinements of the Davis-Whinston method which reduce the ease of cheating and force the cheater to be so cautious as to allow combined profit to nearly reach its maximum. The method Davis and Whinston have given us is potentially important enough to warrant considerable study.

5.2. The "private bargain" solution approach and its drawbacks

As we stated in reviewing the literature in section 1.3, the work of Coase (1960), Turvey (1963), and Buchanan (1966), constitutes a fully decentralized, market approach to the externality question. This approach holds that, since the P.O. outputs are those which maximize combined profit, the firms have incentive to agree to produce the optimal outputs and then distribute the profit such that each firm's profit is greater than or equal to the profit it could earn by maximizing individually. In order for a firm to agree to produce (P.O.) output levels which would not maximize its profit function, it is necessary for payments to be made which induce it to do so. The firm which gains from having P.O. externality levels produced will have to enter a bargain to make payments to the firm which loses. Because P.O. outputs maximize combined profit, such a bargain is always profitable to both firms. There are, of course, many possible bargains since the extra combined profit from producing P.O. outputs can be distributed in many ways.

If the bargain is enforceable at law, the payments need be in no special form. They need only be great enough to make the firm's profit at P.O. output levels and including the payment greater than what the firm could earn without payment but with the outputs which maximize its individual profit function. If the bargain is *not* enforceable at law, then the payments must be of a form to modify the firm's profit function to satisfy conditions (3.3.3) and (3.3.4). This will prevent cheating by the firm.

Those who, from entirely unexceptionable reasoning such as that in the preceding paragraph, would jump to the conclusion that private bargains among firms affected by externalities will *always* result in the production of P.O. output levels without help from the state, should not ignore the insights of game theory into conflict behavior.[13] The difficulties of bargaining in a "cooperative game" situation, where a larger combined profit can be gained by cooperation than by individual action but where there is a conflict of interest in the distribution of that profit, are pointed out in Luce and Raiffa (1957) and Bishop (1963). Game theoretic arguments are used by Wellisz (1964) to show that the bargaining solution breaks down when large groups are involved in the bargain or when the externalities are mutual.

The large-group difficulty lies in that it is to the advantage of any member of the group to refuse to bear any part of the cost of a settlement, while reaping the advantages. If there are n farmers affected by the smoke from a train, it pays any farmer to let the remaining $(n - 1)$ bribe the railway and to enjoy cost-free the results of the bargain.[14]

Wellisz also points out that if there are mutual (nonseparable) externalities among two (or more) firms, neither may be able to find stable output levels maximizing individually, so it may not be possible to determine the size of the payment which would lead to a maximum of combined profit. He leaves the impression that where there are only two firms, one producing and one receiving the externality, the "private bargain" approach works. He is too generous.

We can extend game theoretic arguments to the case of two firms (or a small number) having one-way externalities. If we adopt the "usual" assumptions of game theory, each firm knows the other firm's profit function. While a bargain which can achieve optimal output levels is possible (as in all cases of externalities), the bargain may not actually occur if the participants use the strategy of threats in the bargaining

[13] I may be accused of setting up a straw man by this statement. None of the writers I have cited literally concludes that private bargains will always occur and result in Pareto optimality. However, each of them invites the casual reader to this conclusion. None notes the defects of bargains strongly and implies that they are anything but occasional exceptions. Nor is the need for alternatives usually noted, to handle the cases where bargains do not occur. Of course, one may conclude, on various grounds, that government intervention is ineffective or is less desirable than nonoptimal externality levels. It is fairer to all if that conclusion, and the economic or political reasoning behind it, is made explicit. (Buchanan does this in his 1962 article and in *The Calculus of Consent* [1962], but he does not sufficiently cite this line of reasoning in his 1966 work.)

[14] Wellisz (1964), p. 354.

process. A participant may threaten either to produce a certain output level which would be particularly harmful to the other firm[15] or to not participate at all and maximize in isolation. If it is necessary to carry out the threat—to save face or to make the threat believable the next time around—a nonoptimal bargain will be reached. Most wars and strikes are examples.

If we make the more realistic assumption that neither firm knows with any certainty the other's profit function, then neither firm knows the "best" offer to make the other; an incorrect offer may break down the bargaining (particularly if threat strategies are used) or slow it so that for many periods it is suboptimal.

Furthermore, as Shapley and Shubik (1969) have shown, some external diseconomy games have no "core" (the set of feasible outcomes, none of which can be overturned by any coalition acting in its own interest). In such games, bargain agreements are not stable; some coalition(s) can profitably violate the agreement.

Thus it seems difficult to escape the conclusion that bargaining, whether on the "usual" assumptions of game theory or on the assumption of imperfect knowledge, cannot assure us of a socially optimal solution. Certainly there is more profit to distribute when P.O. output levels are produced than when the firms maximize in isolation. However, the problem of distributing that extra profit breaks down the bargaining process.

It might be argued that the "private bargain" people make no more stringent assumptions than those of perfect competition. That is, the assumption that "rationality will out" (no threat strategies concerning division of a coalition's proceeds will cause the coalition to break down) is no more stringent than the assumptions of perfect competition.

I disagree. The assumptions of perfect competition are stringent and unrealistic concerning the state of the world, but are most hardheaded concerning motivation. People are assumed to rigidly follow self-interest and may use any threat strategies they wish, in order to attain it. However,

---

[15] Wellisz gives an example of such a threat based on Coase's railway example. "To obtain the best bargain with the farmers, the railway might threaten to run five trains per day and thus destroy the entire crop. To avoid this possibility and to obtain a reduction in train runs to two a day, the farmers would be willing to pay . . . the process opens up magnificent business prospects: any activity can be turned to profit as long as it is sufficiently annoying to someone else." (pp. 352, 353)

in perfect competition an individual's threats cannot be effective; therefore they are not used.

If we were to allow the assumptions the "private bargain" people make for externalities to hold everywhere in price theory, we would have no monopoly or imperfect competition theory, and, in fact, no situations anywhere that are not Pareto optimal. After all, the victims of a monopoly could pay the monopolist to act as if he were a perfect competitor and still be better off (by the definition of Pareto optimum). They don't do so, of course, only because bargaining is difficult and breaks down owing to the size of the coalition and/or the issue of division of spoils.[16]

After all, in the real world there *are* externalities among competitive firms, even though bargaining is usually legal. It comes down to this: Are we going to let the real world ruin our nice models? It seems to me that we should incorporate into our models as much of what we know about the world as possible. When useful approximate conclusions can be derived from unrealistic assumptions (such as the assumption of continuity), that is one thing. But when it seems that our unrealistic assumptions will lead us to entirely wrong conclusions, it is time to revise our assumptions. That is why I question the bargaining approach and why I propose "broad" joint production as a model for externalities and propose alternative optimality criteria and pricing models for nonconcave profit functions.

[16] Such phenomena as consumer unions, environmentalist groups, and Ralph Nader can perhaps be thought of as approaches to bargaining with imperfect competitors or externality producers. By exposing a firm's departures from "optimality," they bring pressure on it to lower price, improve the product, or reduce the externality. It would appear that this method of bargaining is used more than, and is probably more effective than, payments to the offending firm.

SIX

Conclusion

In this chapter, I shall summarize and interpret the major analytical results of the book, discuss their applicability to the important public policy issues of dealing with environmental externalities, and outline some of the areas in which further research is most necessary.

TECHNICAL SUMMARY. We deal throughout with a model wherein technological externalities directly affect only the R perfectly competitive firms that make up the production sector. Each of the firms produces one or more saleable commodities and may produce as a by-product one or more externalities which it imposes on the remaining firms as public goods (or "bads"). Externalities affect (for better or worse) the efficiency of the productive resources employed by the recipient firms and are thus only pecuniary externalities to the household or consumption sector. Technological externalities affecting the consumption sector are ruled out so as to avoid problems of utility measurement or interpersonal utility comparisons when Pigovian taxes are calculated.

The traditional model of the production of externalities assumes, not always explicitly, a "strict" joint product production function. The first necessity, therefore, is to derive a production function where the externality is free to vary without being fixed in proportion to some other output or input and where its by-product character is preserved (levels greater than zero exist in laissez-faire equilibrium even though the externality generates no revenue). This is accomplished by deriving production function (2.1.4), a generalization of the "broad" joint product model:

$$F_{i1}(q_i, X_{i1}, v_{i1}^n, v_i^p) = 0$$
$$F_{ik}(x_{i0m}, v_{ik}^n, v_i^p) = 0 \tag{2.1.4}$$

A crucial role in this model is played by the vector of "joint inputs," v_i^p; each element of the vector appears in equation 1 of firm i's production function and in one or more of the other equations in the production set. This accounts for positive levels of externalities in laissez-faire equilibrium and makes it possible for firm i to alter the externality level by reducing a joint input and substituting an ordinary input (an element of v_{i1}^n) for it in equation 1 or allocating positive quantities of ordinary inputs to equation k. Neither of these reallocations necessarily reduces a saleable commodity in proportion to the change in externality level; such proportionality should result only as a matter of technological reality rather than by economic assumption.

Section 2.2 then rigorously derives from this production function a cost function which is later on embodied in the profit function used when we calculate Pigovian taxes and subsidies:

$$P_i = pq_i' - k_i(q_i, X_i) \tag{4.1.1}$$

where P is a vector of market prices of saleable commodities and k_i is the cost function of firm i, which is convex and has continuous first and second partial derivatives if the production function has these properties.

Pareto efficiency conditions for externalities have rarely been explored in the literature and have never been developed using an appropriate production function which differentiates among the (possibly several) firms producing each type of externality. Our criterion for productive sector efficiency (maximize output of one saleable commodity subject to constant total amounts of other saleable commodities and costly inputs) gives us the following conditions involving inputs and externalities:

$$\frac{\partial v_{jkn}}{\partial x_{j0m}} = -\sum_{\substack{i=1 \\ i \neq j,r}}^{R} \frac{\partial v_{iln}}{\partial x_{j0m}} \tag{3.1.12}$$

$$\frac{\partial v_{jp}}{\partial x_{j0m}} = -\sum_{\substack{i=1 \\ i \neq j,r}}^{R} \frac{\partial v_{ip}}{\partial x_{j0m}} \tag{3.1.14}$$

These may be interpreted analogously to the famous Samuelson condition for public goods: the marginal rates of technical substitution between an ordinary input v_n (or a joint input v_p) and the externality x_{j0m} summed over the firms receiving the externality equals the marginal social cost of producing the externality (rate at which a valuable private good must be

125

used to produce the externality). A similar condition can be derived in a graphical analysis that makes use of an open-topped Edgeworth box.

The efficiency conditions result in an infinitude of efficient points. It is proved in section 3.2 that one efficient point is that set of saleable outputs, externalities, and inputs which maximizes combined profit of the firms affected by the externalities. That point has no special welfare significance beyond efficiency because it depends on the initial prices and quantities of outputs and inputs. Also, no claim is made for the optimality of the possible profit distributions resulting from enforcement of this point. (However, allowing side payments, a Pareto optimal profit distribution which preserves each firm's status quo ante is derived in Appendix B.) The rule "maximize combined profit" can also be given an intuitive interpretation. We can reason by extension of the fundamental theorem of welfare economics that when the R firms merge and act like a perfect competitor, maximizing combined profit, the outcome is Pareto optimal (assuming the other firms and consumers in the economy are also acting as competitors).

Until fairly recently, most economists have felt, with Pigou, that a system of taxes and subsidies can be designed which can give firms incentive, in maximizing their own profit, to produce socially optimal levels of externalities and ordinary outputs. Since 1960, tax/subsidy schemes have been attacked for not bringing about the output levels they intend to bring about, and for a narrow, strictly marginal definition of the social optimum. Most recent writers have abandoned Pigovian (centralized) approaches in favor of decentralized solutions. A major goal of this book is to try to right that balance by examining some of the disadvantages of decentralized solutions and by outlining the requirements for an informationally centralized solution that will achieve the goal of P.O. outputs and retain the decisionally decentralized character of the market system.

Thus, the next major part of the book discusses centralized methods of determining generalized joint product "prices" intended to impel the firms to produce P.O. levels of joint products. As the jumping off point for this discussion, we set forth necessary and sufficient conditions for optimal externality "shadow prices." One version of these conditions is completely general and does not depend on the assumptions of concavity and continuity. A useful special case states that an optimal set of assigned prices must modify strictly concave profit functions of the firms so that the modified functions, E_i, meet the following conditions:

(a) $\dfrac{\partial E_i(q_i^*, X_i^*)}{\partial q_{il}} = 0$

$$(3.3.6)$$

(b) $\dfrac{\partial E_i(q_i^*, X_i^*)}{\partial x_{i0m}} = 0$

$$\dfrac{\partial E_i(q_i^*, X_i^*)}{\partial x_{j0m}} = 0 \qquad (3.3.7)$$

These conditions state that each firm must, when assigned optimal "prices," want to produce P.O. levels of outputs under its control (q_{il} and x_{i0m}) and must want each other firm to produce P.O. levels of outputs that affect it (x_{j0m}).

Pigovian taxes and subsidies are special cases of externality shadow prices and must satisfy the conditions just set forth. Section 3.4 shows that the "standard" Pigovian schemes proposed to date fail to meet these conditions. Section 4.1 then develops a generalized joint product pricing algorithm which does meet these conditions. The matrix of optimal joint product prices relevant to firm i is

$$C_i^* = \dfrac{\partial k_i(q_i^*, X_i^*)}{\partial X_i} \qquad (4.1.8)$$

An element (c_{i0m}^*) of the matrix C_i^* may be the Pigovian tax or subsidy on firm i's output of externality m. It is proved in section 4.2 that these prices do indeed meet the conditions of section 3.3. Section 4.5 deals with non-separable cost functions, where the level of a firm's own outputs which maximizes its individual profit depends on the level of the externality set by another firm. It is shown that the fact that the prices, C_i^*, satisfy conditions (3.3.6) and (3.3.7) implies that each firm has all the information necessary to predict the externality levels the other firms whose externalities affect it will set and that the prediction will be self-fulfilling. There is no incentive for one firm to trick any other firm into producing non-P.O. outputs. Such outputs would be achieved only *temporarily* as the result of *unsuccessful* blackmail. Successful blackmail will result in P.O. outputs. It is interesting but rather extraneous to note that there also exists an iterative process where each firm estimates (and continually re-estimates) the other firms' outputs. This will usually result in outputs converging on

127

the P.O. if for some reason one firm chooses not to use the information that the externality levels it *wants* other firms to set are the levels they actually *will* set.

A generalization of the transfer price problem of managerial economics is set forth in section 4.3, using the production function and shadow price algorithm developed for externalities. Intermediate products transferred among divisions of a large firm are treated as private good joint products, and externalities among divisions are treated as public good joint products. Several theorems are proved for externalities in section 4.2 and several others for transfer prices in 4.3. Together, they constitute a proof of quantity-price duality between private and public production goods. It is shown in section 4.4 that this extends the duality between public and private consumption goods noted by Samuelson (1955) to production goods and to quantity-price in addition to quantity-*MRS* relations— whose duality for production goods is already implicit in (3.1.12). The quantity-price duality relations are:

Transferred products—private goods:

$$x_{i \cdot m} = \sum_j x_{ijm} \qquad (j = 1, \ldots, R, \neq i)$$

$$\{c^*_{ijm}\}_i = \{c^*_{ijm}\}_j = c^*_{i1m}$$

$$= c^*_{i2m} = \cdots$$

$$= c^*_{iRm} \qquad (j = 1, \ldots, R, \neq i) \qquad \text{(Th. 5, 7)}$$

Externalities—public goods:

$$\{x_{i0m}\}_i = \{x_{i0m}\}_j \qquad (j = 1, \ldots, R, \neq i)$$

$$c^*_{i0m} = - \sum_j c^*_{ijm} \qquad (j = 1, \ldots, R, \neq i) \qquad \text{(Th. 2)}$$

(The $\cdot$ in the position of j signifies that $x_{i \cdot m}$ is the amount of the transferred product produced by i and transferred to all the other firms. The notation $\{ \ \}_i$ means "as computed in i's profit function.") Theorem 5, the first two terms of the combined transfer price relation above, is fundamentally a proof that the transfer pricing algorithm really defines a price system, that is, a system with the property that a single price will clear the market. Theorem 7, the remaining terms, states that if an intermediate product is transferred to several divisions, the transfer price to each division

in this book excludes any degree of monopoly behavior by firms. Unless we are prepared to correct both monopoly and externality divergences from optimality together, the theorem of "second best" tells us that we cannot be sure that externality taxes bring about a welfare improvement. Wellisz (1964) and Buchanan (1969) show that externality taxes on monopolists may result in inefficiently restricted output and increase the welfare loss. This conclusion, derived using the traditional model that requires output to fall in a one-to-one functional relationship with the externality, is greatly weakened when the generalized joint product model is applied. With this model, the monopolist will be stimulated to substitute "cleaner" inputs, etc., instead of reducing output precipitously. If we could measure it, we might find that the welfare gain from reducing the external diseconomy often exceeded the incremental welfare loss from a further restriction of output over the laissez-faire monopoly solution. This intuition, which we cannot really prove, should apply even more strongly to regulated monopolies like public utilities.

Despite the differences between the assumptions of my model and the real world, I think it is necessary to comment on its possible policy implications to avoid letting policy decisions go by default to those who would impose quantity restrictions (zoning, outright bans, etc.) or to those who would trust solely to "corporate responsibility." The former solution may be effective but inefficient, and the latter may be ineffective in some cases and improper in others. As Milton Friedman points out, expecting a businessman to go against his economic self-interest invites him to make public policy with only the vaguest mandate and instructions from the public. We have devised a political process, however imperfect, for making public policy decisions; we should not lightly discard it and set the fox to guard the chicken coop. It seems to me that if businessmen want to exercise social responsibility they should argue for externality taxes as the solution most consistent with representative government and private enterprise. Once taxes have been set, there need be no conflict between a businessman's social and his corporate conscience.

In the introduction to this book, I cited two policy issues to which this work may be relevant. The first was whether we must give up a growth economy in order to make meaningful reductions in environmental externalities. This book does not provide a definitive answer because the question is more technological than economic. However, the more realistic production function model of externalities formulated here permits us to address the technological question without the blinders of the built-in pessimistic assumption implied by the traditional model. Also, by identifying joint inputs and ordinary inputs, it invites us to focus on the full range of technical substitution possibilities and their economic feasibility. By giving each firm multiple potential externality production possibilities, it invites us also to consider the danger of "environmental kickback," where the measures adopted to correct one externality cause another.

The second policy question cited in the introduction was whether a tax on the quantity of pollutants can be effective, to whom it should be paid, and whether it should be the same for all producers of the pollutant. Some definite conclusions can be drawn. The taxing scheme worked out in chapter 4 would indeed be a tax on the physical quantity (pounds per hour, cubic meters of water raised x degrees in temperature per hour, etc.) of a particular pollutant. If correctly calculated, it would, in all circumstances, give each firm sufficient incentive to produce the optimal quantity of the pollutant determined by the taxing authority. This conclusion holds whether the externality affects only firms or both consumers and firms; in the latter case, it is only the determination of what is an optimal pollutant quantity that is altered, not the enforcement mechanism.

On the question of to whom the tax should be paid, both the externalities literature and what I have said so far in this book may give a misleading impression. The impression given is that the producer must pay a tax, c_{iim}^* (in general, different for each j), to each firm $j = 1, \ldots, R, \neq i$, (or, by extension, each consumer) affected by the externality. Otherwise, the recipient will have an incentive to bribe the producer to alter his output levels away from the optimum. Such a tax scheme would usually be very difficult to administer and probably cost more than the welfare saving. For example, the quantity of sulfur dioxide from Con Ed's East Side plant reaching me in Greenwich Village each year is so small that the optimal tax I should receive might be less than the bookkeeping cost of paying it. This is certainly true for a smaller polluter, like a fleet of five taxicabs. Fortunately, when there are many recipients of an externality and they are *not* paid the tax, it is not possible for any one of them, or even a manageable coalition, to bribe the polluter enough to alter his externality output away from the optimal. Only a coalition of appreciable size would gain enough from a reduction of pollution below the optimal to pay Con Ed enough to make the reduction. Their action would be visible and could be prevented by law.

Theorem 3 of chapter 4 showed that the same unit tax should be placed on all producers of an identical externality (even though the cost functions of the producers might be different). Externalities produced by several firms are "identical" only when the effect on each recipient of an increment of the externality measured at the source is the same for all producers. Many environmental externalities will not be identical by this definition because of the effect of distance differentials between sources and recipient.

One of the strongest conclusions implicit in the externality tax algorithm, (4.1.8), is the need to devise a complete system of taxes on all interconnected externalities instead of calculating piecemeal taxes. Of course, this is just an application of the "second best" theorem, but it must be emphasized. Serious error will result if we rush ahead and put taxes on a few pollutants and ignore others. For example, a tax on phosphates in laundry detergents will (quite properly) raise the price of these detergents and cause substitution of other detergents and substitution of paper towels and diapers, and the like, for now-more-expensive-to-wash cloth ones. The disposal of waste paper will increase inefficiently unless a tax has also been placed on paper. Piecemeal taxes may also cause manufacturers to switch from one pollutant to another. (Public pressure against phosphates has already caused some manufacturers to substitute carbon compounds which result in eutrophication of rivers and lakes.) One may ask how the government can anticipate every possible aspect of "environmental kickback" before it happens. Of course it cannot, but if it enacts a reasonably comprehensive set of taxes and gives clear evidence of reacting quickly to newly discovered externalities, it will be in the self-interest of firms to investigate carefully the results of any substitution of inputs so as to avoid the expense of retooling at a later date.

It has often been stated that a significant contribution to the problem of pollution, for example "eye-pollution" from scrap metal junkyards, might be made by the recycling of wastes, whether they be gaseous, liquid, or solid. The laissez-faire market system, however, provides a rather weak and unstable incentive for recycling. For example, the price of steel scrap has fluctuated widely and has been rather low in recent years, because of the introduction of the basic oxygen furnace which can accept little scrap. Without interfering with scrap prices as an efficient allocator of resources, we can bring greater incentive to the recycling industry by enacting taxes on scrap as a pollutant. If the person or firm responsible for disposing of waste with steel content in an "eye-polluting manner" is charged a tax which will be refunded if he sells the waste to a recycling firm, the cost of scrap as an input to the recycling process will fall and perhaps even become negative. Without the tax, the lower limit on input prices of the waste recycling industry cannot be much below zero. The tax will thus increase the incentive for recycling.

RESEARCH PRIORITIES. The theorem of "second best" has severely limited the realism of our conclusions several times in this book. Whenever there is any degree of imperfect competition or any doubt as to the accuracy of information reaching the taxing authority, we cannot be sure that the taxes assigned will actually bring about an increase in "welfare." All the exercises of welfare economics, even the economist's traditional distaste for monopolistic practices and restraints on foreign trade, implicitly assume that corrective measures "usually make things better off." But when do they and when don't they? Clearly, a method of testing whether corrective measures are really helpful in an imperfect world ought to be the most important business of welfare theory.

Although many of the conclusions of this book will continue to be valid for externalities affecting consumers as well as firms, the tax-calculating algorithm, in particular, should be formally extended to consumers so that we may face squarely the inherent conceptual and empirical difficulties. When we convert into dollars the "marginal evaluations" of consumers, there is some contradiction to be resolved, for we accept the influence of the existing income distribution on marginal evaluations, while at the same time modifying that income distribution by setting externality taxes.

Decentralized tax-calculating schemes also deserve a great deal more research. If one can be found that prevents or even significantly limits "cheating" by affected firms or consumers, it would be preferable to centralized schemes for many reasons. I am not really optimistic about the possibilities, though. The unwillingness of recipients of a public good to make known what it is worth to them (the "free rider" problem) does not seem to be easily surmountable. It may be that centrally computed taxes based on imperfect estimates may move us farther toward welfare optimality in most cases.

134

Finally, there is a need for a great deal of empirical research on the production and "consumption" of externalities. Attempts should be made to describe and quantify actual externality production and / or cost functions. In particular, the possibilities of input substitution for altering externality levels and the other externalities which may result should be studied in concrete situations. The groundwork for this is being laid by the firms and government agencies studying pollution abatement technology, and the results should soon begin to enter the economic literature. Dollar estimates of the damage (in the broadest possible sense) done to consumers and firms by different levels of each type of pollutant must also be made before taxes can be calculated. (This area has by no means been left untouched by economists, but a great deal still needs to be done.) An incentive for performing these studies and a partial test of the validity and cost of externality taxes might be provided by a government-sponsored pilot run of actual taxes in one area for a small group of interrelated pollutants. We must begin to experiment with externality taxes before other modes of control become too firmly entrenched in our economic system or the problem of pollution itself gets too far out of hand.

135

APPENDIX A: DEMONSTRATION THAT OUTPUTS WHICH MAXIMIZE INDIVIDUAL (PRE-TAX) PROFIT VIOLATE THE PARETO EFFICIENCY CRITERION WHEN EXTERNALITIES ARE PRESENT

We define firm j's "profit" or net rent as in equation (3.2.1):

$$P_j = \sum_{l=1}^{L} p_l q_{jl} - \sum_{n=1}^{N} \sum_{k=1}^{K} w_n v_{jkn} - \sum_{p=1}^{P} w_p v_{jp} + \sum_{k=1}^{K} \lambda_{jk} F_{jk} \qquad (A.1)$$

The first-order conditions for a maximum of P_j are

$$\frac{\partial P_j}{\partial q_{jl}} = p_l + \lambda_{j1} \frac{\partial F_{j1}}{\partial q_{jl}} = 0 \qquad\qquad (l = 1, \ldots, L) \qquad (A.2)$$

$$\frac{\partial P_j}{\partial v_{jkn}} = -w_n + \lambda_{jk} \frac{\partial F_{jk}}{\partial v_{jkn}} = 0 \qquad\qquad \begin{array}{l} (n = 1, \ldots, N \\ k = 1, \ldots, K) \end{array} \qquad (A.3)$$

$$\frac{\partial P_j}{\partial v_{jp}} = -w_p + \sum_{k=1}^{K} \lambda_{jk} \frac{\partial F_{jk}}{\partial v_{jp}} = 0 \qquad\qquad (p = 1, \ldots, P) \qquad (A.4)$$

$$\frac{\partial P_j}{\partial x_{j0m}} = \lambda_{jk} \frac{\partial F_{jk}}{\partial x_{j0m}} = 0 \qquad\qquad \begin{array}{l} (m = 1, \ldots, M \\ k = m + 1) \end{array} \qquad (A.5)^1$$

$$\frac{\partial P_j}{\partial \lambda_{jk}} = F_{jk} = 0 \qquad\qquad (k = 1, \ldots, K) \qquad (A.6)$$

[1] Firm j maximizes its profit with respect to the x_{i0m}, the externalities under its control. If F_{j1} is nonseparable, the level of the x_{i0m}, the externalities produced by other firms, will affect the optimal level of all the variables under firm j's control and firm j will have to estimate values for the x_{i0m} and plug them into F_{j1} in equations (A.2)–(A.4). Firm j will never differentiate with respect to the x_{i0m} since it cannot set their levels.

We shall derive the multiplier-free first-order condition involving v_{jkn} and x_{j0m} and compare it to the analogous Pareto efficiency condition

$$\frac{\partial v_{jkn}}{\partial x_{j0m}} = - \sum_{\substack{i=1 \\ i \neq j,r}}^{R} \frac{\partial v_{i1n}}{\partial x_{j0m}} \tag{3.1.12}$$

Solving (A.3) for λ_{jk}, substituting in (A.5), and applying the implicit function theorem, we get one of firm j's profit-maximizing conditions in terms of v_{jkn} and x_{j0m}:

$$\frac{\partial v_{jkn}}{\partial x_{j0m}} = - \frac{1}{w_p} \tag{A.7}$$

Since there is no reason why the quantity $-1/w_p$, determined in the marketplace, should equal the quantity $-\sum_i \partial v_{i1n}/\partial x_{j0m}$ in the Pareto efficiency conditions, we conclude that externality levels which satisfy the conditions for maximum P_j will not generally be those which satisfy the Pareto efficiency conditions. This result has of course been proved before, but not by direct application of the Pareto criterion.

APPENDIX B: PROOF THAT OUTPUTS WHICH GIVE A PARETO OPTIMAL PROFIT DISTRIBUTION AMONG R FIRMS EXPERIENCING EXTERNALITIES ARE ALSO PARETO EFFICIENT AND MAXIMIZE COMBINED PROFIT OF THE R FIRMS

In this section, we apply the Pareto criterion to the *profit* of R firms experiencing production externalities, increasing the profit of one firm while holding the profit of the other firms at some fixed, feasible level. We can, without loss of generality, increase firm 1's profit, say, while holding the profits of firms $i = 2, \ldots, R$ at the fixed levels, $\bar{P}_i$ (we may set the $\bar{P}_i$ at zero or at the individual maximum which was attained before central intervention, or at some other level—the optimal outputs will be the same). We allow for side payments s_i $(i = 2, \ldots, R)$ from firm 1 to each of the other firms so that 1 may be completely free in setting variable level so as to maximize its profit subject to the constraint.

Maximize

$$P_1 = \sum_{l=1}^{L} p_l q_{1l} - \sum_{n=1}^{N} \sum_{k=1}^{K} w_n v_{1kn} - \sum_{p=1}^{P} w_p v_{1p}$$

$$+ \sum_{k=1}^{K} \lambda_{1k} F_{1k} - \sum_{i=2}^{R} s_i + \sum_{i=2}^{R} \sigma_i$$

$$\times \left[\sum_{l=1}^{L} p_l q_{il} - \sum_{n=1}^{N} \sum_{k=1}^{K} w_n v_{ikn} \right.$$

$$\left. - \sum_{p=1}^{P} w_p v_{ip} + \sum_{k=1}^{K} \lambda_{ik} F_{ik} + s_i - \bar{P}_i \right] \tag{B.1}$$

139

Setting the first partial derivatives equal to zero, we get

$$\frac{\partial P_1}{\partial q_{il}} = \sigma_i \left[p_l + \lambda_{i1} \frac{\partial F_{i1}}{\partial q_{il}} \right] = 0 \qquad \begin{matrix} (i = 1, \ldots, R \\ l = 1, \ldots, L) \end{matrix} \qquad (B.2)^1$$

$$\frac{\partial P_1}{\partial v_{ikn}} = \sigma_i \left[-w_n + \lambda_{ik} \frac{\partial F_{ik}}{\partial v_{ikn}} \right] = 0 \qquad \begin{matrix} (i = 1, \ldots, R \\ k = 1, \ldots, K \\ n = 1, \ldots, N) \end{matrix} \qquad (B.3)$$

$$\frac{\partial P_1}{\partial v_{ip}} = \sigma_i \left[-w_p + \sum_{k=1}^{K} \lambda_{ik} \frac{\partial F_{ik}}{\partial v_{ip}} \right] = 0 \qquad \begin{matrix} (i = 1, \ldots, R \\ p = 1, \ldots, P) \end{matrix} \qquad (B.4)$$

$$\frac{\partial P_1}{\partial x_{j0m}} = \sum_{i=1}^{R \neq j} \sigma_i \left[\lambda_{i1} \frac{\partial F_{i1}}{\partial x_{j0m}} \right] + \sigma_j \lambda_{jk} \frac{\partial F_{jk}}{\partial x_{j0m}} = 0$$

$$\begin{matrix} (j = 1, \ldots, R \\ m = 1, \ldots, M \\ k = m + 1) \end{matrix} \qquad (B.5)$$

$$\frac{\partial P_1}{\partial \lambda_{ik}} = \sigma_i F_{ik} = 0 \qquad \begin{matrix} (i = 1, \ldots, R \\ k = 1, \ldots, K) \end{matrix} \qquad (B.6)$$

$$\frac{\partial P_1}{\partial \sigma_i} = \sum_{l=1}^{L} p_l q_{il} - \sum_{n=1}^{N} \sum_{k=1}^{K} w_n v_{ikn} - \sum_{p=1}^{P} w_p v_{ip} + \sum_{k=1}^{K} \lambda_{ik} F_{ik}$$

$$+ s_i - \bar{P}_i = 0 \qquad (i = 2, \ldots, R) \qquad (B.7)$$

$$\frac{\partial P_1}{\partial s_i} = -1 + \sigma_i = 0 \qquad (i = 2, \ldots, R) \qquad (B.8)$$

From (B.8) we find that $\sigma_i = 1$ for $i = 2, \ldots, R$ and substitute for σ_i in the other equations. Equations (B.2)–(B.6) are now identical to equations (3.2.2)–(3.2.6), the first-order conditions for maximizing combined profit. By appropriate choice of the s_i, variables which satisfy (B.2)–(B.6) will also satisfy (B.7) so the latter equation set does not constrain the solution. Thus we have proved that the same unique set of variables which maximizes combined profit of R firms experiencing production externalities will also give a Pareto optimal profit distribution with the choice of appropriate side payments. By the proof in sections 3.1 and 3.2, these variables will meet the conditions for Pareto efficiency as well.

[1] We allow i to cover the range $1, \ldots, R$ for compactness. When $i = 1$ we assume $\sigma_i = 1$. Thus

$$\frac{\partial P_1}{\partial q_{1l}} = p_l + \lambda_{11} \frac{\partial F_{11}}{\partial q_{1l}} = 0.$$

The same assumption will be used in equations (B.3)–(B.6).

APPENDIX C: NON-CONVEX EXTERNALITY COST FUNCTIONS

This section considers the implications of the idea, first suggested to me by Professor Vickrey of Columbia, that non-convex externality cost functions (which imply non-concave profit functions) of one or more recipient firms mean that the prices C_i^* of (4.1.9) do *not* ensure that P.O. outputs are achieved. It is shown here that for this case, the prices C_i^* meet conditions (3.3.3) and (3.3.5) but violate the fundamental condition, (3.3.4). A (somewhat *ad hoc*) piecewise linear "price" function is then derived which meets condition (3.3.4). It is shown that this scheme is a generalization of the method of equations (4.1.9).

It is usually reasonable to expect cost functions to be convex over their economically relevant range because of the assumption of diminishing returns to all inputs, including externalities. The assumption is not always justified for externalities, however. The cost function of firm i may not be convex with respect to an externality imposed on it by another firm. The type of cost curve and the isocost and isoquant shapes implied by it are shown in Figure C-1.

In panel (a) (ignore the line labeled $c_{21}^* x_2$ for the moment), we see that, in the range above $\hat{x}_2$, a line connecting any two points on k_1 will not be always above the curve; thus that portion of k_1 is non-convex. In panel (b), we note that below $\hat{x}_2$, as you increase x_2, q_1 has to decrease at a growing rate in order to maintain k_1. Above $\hat{x}_2$, increases in x_2 result in decreases in q_1 but at a falling rate, possibly reaching a point where x_2 can increase without bound without reducing q_1. Similarly, in panel (c), below $\hat{x}_2$, as we increase x_2, it takes increasingly more v_1 (input) to maintain q_1. Above $\hat{x}_2$, it takes decreasingly more.

Cost functions like this are theoretically possible, although by no means exclusively the case, for externality problems. Non-convex cost functions *result when it is feasible, above a certain level of externality, to adjust the method of production so that the externality no longer affects certain factors of production.*[1] For example, suppose we have a laundry affected by smoke. If the factor v_1 is labor, as smoke increases it takes more labor to rewash laundry soiled by hanging in smoky air. Above some level of the externality, it may be feasible to allocate some labor to build a roof or erect a tent. If we wish to keep our curves continuous, we may visualise the labor as erecting the roof board by board, gradually reducing the effect of the externality. More likely, of course, the function will be

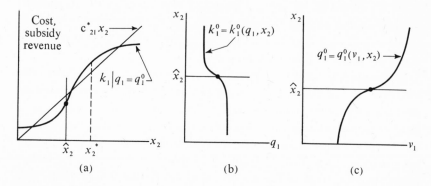

(a)   (b)   (c)

FIGURE C-1

Non-convex externality total cost, isocost, and isoquant curves for recipient

discontinuous at one or several points. Alternatively, a change in technique may involve a capital expenditure. Installing electric dryers, for example, could reduce v_1 as x_2 increases, although of course, expenditure on all resources should continue to increase.

Failure of the solution proposed in section 4.1. We can present the elements of the solution proposed in section 4.1 by using Figure C-1. This figure assumes a two-firm model where firm 2 produces an external diseconomy which it imposes on 1. The outputs q_1^*, q_2^*, and x_2^*, which

[1] Buchanan and Stubblebine (1962), p. 377, give an example of a consumer's utility function non-concave for the same reason. Their example is of a fence erected by B, which, to a certain height gives A privacy but above a certain height blocks his view. Finally, a height is reached where A's view is completely blocked and additions to the fence don't further affect his utility. The authors do not extend this reasoning to consider its effect on tax/subsidy schemes however. Professor Vickrey seems to have been the first to consider this. It will be explored in this section.

maximize combined profit of the two firms, are the P.O. outputs. If firm 2's cost function and firm 1's cost function in the direction of the q_1 axis are convex, we can find the optimal "price," c_{21}^*, by the method of section 4.1. In terms of Figure C-1, that method sets the charge such that c_{21}^* equals the slope of k_1 at x_2^*, the derivative $\partial k_1/\partial x_2$ evaluated at q_1^*, x_2^*.

If k_1 is convex, this procedure ensures that firm 1's subsidy revenue $c_{21}^* x_2$, exceeds k_1 by the greatest amount at this point (or falls short of k_1 by the smallest amount at this point), and thus firm 1 will want firm 2 to set $x_2 = x_2^*$. However, we see in Figure C-1 that we get a (local, at least) *minimum* net of subsidy revenue over cost at x_2^*. We see that in this case firm 1 would want firm 2 to increase x_2 toward infinity as that would increase 1's profit without bound.

In this example (and for separable cost functions generally), firm 1 has no better choice than to accept x_2^* and produce q_1^* because the initial post-tax solution is completely acceptable to firm 2. Firm 1 would pay 2 to alter x_2, but it cannot offer enough to make firm 2 accept because the values q_1^*, q_2^*, and x_2^* maximize combined profit after taxes (because the tax on 2 cancels with the subsidy to 1, giving us the pre-tax combined profit function from which we originally found the P.O. values). Any other values would cause 2 to lose more than 1 would gain. The same holds for nonseparable cost functions.

However, there is no unique value of x_2 which the optimal charge will lead firm 1 to predict (in Figure C-1, there are two levels of x_2 which meet the first-derivative condition, and one—the wrong one—which meets the second-derivative test). If the cost function is nonseparable, firm 1 may set a non-P.O. level of a variable whose profit-maximizing level depends on x_2. If firm 2's decision as to the level of x_2 then depends on the level of a variable under 1's control (mutual, nonseparable externalities) and its cost function is non-convex with respect to that variable, it may not predict that variable correctly.

Then, if the iterative process described in section 4.5 does not converge, the P.O. output levels will be achieved only if the firms cooperate in setting them by exchanging information as to the (P.O.) level at which each would like to set its variable. And there is nothing to guarantee that one firm may not prefer the non-P.O. levels that would exist if it refuses to give information. (For example, 1's gain if 2 sets $x_2 \neq x_2^*$ may exceed its loss when it decides as a result to set $x_1 \neq x_1^*$.) The fact that combined profit is at a maximum at P.O. output levels does not necessarily imply that each firm's is.[2] Now it may be that this combination of unfortunate circumstances is very unlikely, but it is possible and we should consider how to handle it.

Externality "prices" C_i^* meet condition (3.3.5) *but violate condition* (3.3.4). If we assume that the cost function of firm i is convex except with respect to an externality imposed on it by another firm, then we can find the "prices" in the usual way (equation 4.1.8). They will modify the profit function of firm i so that

(a) (3.3.3) holds and firm i maximizes its profit by producing the P.O. level of each output under its control. (The derivatives $\partial E_i/\partial q_i$ and $\partial E_i/\partial X_i^o$ [X_i^o defined to exclude x_{j0m}] equal zero when evaluated at the P.O. values, and, because they are monotonically decreasing, guarantee a maximum of profit.)

(b) (3.3.5) holds and no coalition of firms can afford to pay firm j to alter $x_{j0m} = x_{j0m}^*$. (As was argued above, the P.O. values maximize after tax combined profit so any other value of x_{j0m} would cause firm j to lose more than the other firms could gain from the change.)

(c) (3.3.4) does not hold. Firm i's profit will *in*crease if there is any change away from the P.O. level of x_{j0m}.

It was noted in section 3.3 that (3.3.5), which was derived from (3.3.4), is, together with (3.3.3), only a necessary condition for optimal "prices." Now we see why. These conditions are met when we apply the "prices" C_i^* defined by (4.1.8) to problems with non-convex cost functions of the type described here and yet the "prices" do not enforce the P.O. outputs in all circumstances. Clearly, condition (3.3.4) is also necessary—and since it implies (3.3.5) that condition is not really needed.

Conditions (3.3.3) and (3.3.4) are the minimal necessary and sufficient conditions for optimal assigned prices in the following sense: if and only if these conditions hold can we be sure that the assigned price function that makes them hold can enforce P.O. outputs for *any* cost function.[3] Each firm will choose P.O. levels of outputs under its control and wish each

[2] Naturally, the firms could, by a bargaining process involving payments, achieve P.O. outputs, just as they could before taxes, but this process cannot be guaranteed to work, as is shown in section 5.2.

[3] For separable cost functions *only*, (3.3.3) and (3.3.5) are necessary and sufficient and (3.3.4) is not necessary.

from Figures C-1 and C-2, may not be the same amount. There should be a way to explain this directly, without having to use condition (3.3.5).

A trivial nonlinear solution. The scheme about to be presented is so trivial that it says more about the artificiality of the whole tax/subsidy approach than I would want to say. However, it works, and has not to my knowledge been proposed before. This scheme is simply to credit each firm with a subsidy function equal to the sum of the profit functions of each other firm. This transforms each firm's pre-subsidy profit function into a post-subsidy profit function equal to the combined profit function. Naturally, the profit-maximizing outputs of each firm are the P.O. outputs whatever the shape of the cost functions. One disadvantage of this scheme is that each firm is given information about the other firms that is perhaps none of its business. It also gives huge subsidies to the firms and would drain the coffers of any government and result in great redistributions of income. These problems are avoided by the two-price solution proposed earlier.

We can conclude from this section that, for continuous cost functions, whether they be convex or not, the generalization (C.1) of the pricing algorithm (4.1.8) can give firms, in maximizing their individual profit, incentive to produce socially optimal levels of generalized joint products.

APPENDIX D: THE "BAUMOL PROBLEM"—
VIOLATION OF THE SECOND-ORDER
CONDITIONS FOR A SOCIAL
WELFARE MAXIMUM

Baumol (1964) drew the important conclusion that the presence of externalities can cause the second-order conditions for a maximum of social welfare to be violated. In this section, we shall first apply Baumol's analysis to the case of production externalities, where the analogous result is that the second-order conditions for a maximum of *combined profit* are violated. Then we shall show that this can happen *only* when an *individual* firm profit function is non-concave. An individual firm profit function can be non-concave because of nondiminishing returns to increases of the externality level of some other firm (as we showed in Appendix C) or because of the size of the nonseparable term in the profit function. The former implies that the combined profit function can also be non-concave because of nondiminishing returns, a case Baumol did not consider. We conclude that one must be cautious in the application of classical maximization techniques and in the use of theoretical conclusions arrived at using the calculus. This is not a cause for despair, however; other methods of analysis are available, as we have shown in section 3.3 and Appendix C.

Baumol assumed a social welfare function, W, which is the sum of the individual welfare functions of the units affected by externalities.[1] This, of course, is analogous to the results we proved in section 3.2. It was shown there that P.O. outputs are those outputs which maximize combined profit, the sum of the individual profit functions of the firms affected by production externalities. The "Baumol problem" for production externalities is that combined profit may be of such a form that when we use

[1] He noted in a footnote that the same results could be proved for a social welfare function which is an increasing function of each individual welfare function.

148

the calculus to try to find its maximum, we get a saddle point instead. This does *not* mean that there is no maximum; it only means that we cannot find the maximum by classical optimization techniques. It also means that whatever theoretical conclusions we arrived at using the calculus are not valid for this type of profit function. It is important to note that there are other methods of analysis, such as those used in Appendix C and section 3.3.

Let us assume a simple model of the type of (1.3.1) and examine the ways in which the second-order conditions can be violated. P^i is the profit of firm i. P_i is the derivative of P with respect to variable i.

$$P^1 = f^1(q_1, q_2); \qquad P^2 = f^2(q_2, q_1)$$

$$\text{maximize } P = P^1 + P^2 = f^1(q_1, q_2) + f^2(q_2, q_1) \qquad \text{(D.1)}$$

The second-order conditions for a maximum of P are

$$\text{a. } P_{ii} < 0; \qquad \text{b. } P_{11}P_{22} > (P_{12})^2 \qquad \text{(D.2)}$$

These conditions are violated in two cases. First, if P_{11} and P_{22} are not both less than zero, that is, if there are not diminishing returns with respect to both output levels. Second, if $(P_{12})^2$ is greater than the absolute value of $P_{11}P_{22}$.[2]

Baumol considered only the second case; he did not allow for the case of nondiminishing returns (possibly because that is usually rejected in price theory).

To go deeper into the "Baumol problem," let us analyze what kind of *individual firm* profit functions are implied by a combined profit function that violates the second-order conditions for a maximum. These conditions can only be violated if the combined profit function is not concave over at least some part of its range. Now we know that the sum of concave functions is concave. Therefore, if the function $P (= P^1 + P^2)$ is non-concave, it can only be because one of the functions P^1, P^2 is non-concave. *Every "Baumol problem" must be accompanied by (in fact arises from) a problem where an individual firm profit function is non-concave.*

Appendix C considered the case where the individual firm cost function is non-convex, which means that the profit function is non-concave. We argued that there are economically realistic cases where we cannot assume

[2] This case can happen only with nonseparable externalities since with separable externalities the terms of P_1 do not contain q_2 and vice versa; thus the terms of P_{12} are zero. Baumol assumed only nonseparable externalities anyway.

diminishing returns with respect to increases of the externality. This implies that P_{jj}^i can be greater than zero. Thus it seems that the assumption of diminishing returns is not always justified for combined profit functions, either. If P_{jj}^i is greater than zero, it can happen (depending on P^j) that P_{jj} may also be greater than zero.[3] Baumol did not consider this case, but the analysis here shows that it is possible.

P^i may also be non-concave if $(P_{ij}^i)^2$ is greater than the absolute value of $P_{ii}^i P_{jj}^i$. This can happen if a nonseparable term of P^i (a term involving q_i and q_j) is sufficiently large. Appendix C did not consider this case, but it is clearly worthy of mention, particularly considering the emphasis Baumol gave it. This entire area of nonseparability, its relation to non-concavity, and the convergence questions of sections 4.5 and 5.1 relating to it bear deeper study than this book has been able to give it.

Again, it should be pointed out that the fact that individual or combined profit functions may sometimes be non-concave is no cause to reject all the analysis that has been done on externalities. It simply indicates that we should be cautious in using the calculus in our analysis of externality problems. We should build up a parallel analysis that does not depend on the concavity assumption (or on continuity either, hopefully) as I have tried to do, *partially*, in section 3.3 and Appendix C.

---

[3] We note that, while non-concavity of P implies that P^i or P^j must be non-concave, the converse is not necessarily true: P^i or P^j may be non-concave and P may still be concave.

BIBLIOGRAPHY

Apostol, T. M. (1957). *Mathematical Analysis.* Reading, Mass.: Addison-Wesley.

Ayres, R. V., and A. V. Kneese (1969), "Production, Consumption, and Externalities," *American Economic Review*, Vol. 54, No. 3 (June 1969), pp. 282–297.

Bator, Francis M. (1958). "The Anatomy of Market Failure," *Quarterly Journal of Economics* (August 1958), pp. 351–379.

Baumol, W. J. (1964). "External Economies and Second-Order Optimality Conditions," *American Economic Review*, Vol. LIV, No. 4 (June 1964), pp. 358–372.

——, and T. Fabian (1964). "Decomposition, Pricing for Decentralization, and External Economies," *Management Science*, Vol. 11 (September 1964), pp. 1–33.

Bishop, R. L. (1963). "Game Theoretic Analyses of Bargaining," *Quarterly Journal of Economics*, Vol. 77 (November 1963).

Buchanan, J. M. (1962). "Policy and the Pigovian Margins," *Economica*, Vol. 29 (February 1962).

——, (1966). "Joint Supply, Externality, and Optimality," *Economica* (November 1966).

——, (1969). "External Diseconomies, Corrective Taxes, and Market Structure," *American Economic Review*, Vol. 59, No. 1 (March 1969).

——, and W. C. Stubblebine (1962). "Externality," *Economica* (November 1962).

——, and Gordon M. Tullock (1962). *The Calculus of Consent: Logical Foundations of Constitutional Democracy.* Ann Arbor, Mich.: University of Michigan Press.

Carlson, Sune (1939). *The Pure Theory of Production.* London: P. S. King and Son.

Coase, R. H. (1960). "The Problem of Social Cost," *Journal of Law and Economics*, Vol. 3 (October 1960).

Cook, P. W. (1955). "Decentralization and the Transfer Price Problem," *Journal of Business* (April 1955).

Danø, Sven (1966). *Industrial Production Models—A Theoretical Study.* Københavns Universitets Økonomiske Institut. Vienna–New York: Springer-Verlag.

151

Davis, O. A., and A. B. Whinston (1962). "Externalities, Welfare, and the Theory of Games," *Journal of Political Economy*, Vol. 70 (June 1962).

——, (1965). "Welfare Economics and the Theory of Second Best," *Review of Economic Studies* (January 1965), pp. 1–14.

—— (1966). "On Externalities, Information, and the Government-Assisted Invisible Hand," *Economica* (August 1966).

—— (1967). "Piecemeal Policy in the Theory of Second Best," *Review of Economic Studies*, Vol. XXXIV (3), No. 99 (July 1967), pp. 323–331.

Dolbear, F. T., Jr. (1967). "On the Theory of Optimum Externality," *American Economic Review*, Vol. LVII, No. 1 (March 1967).

Frisch, Ragnar (1965). *Theory of Production*. Dordrecht: Reidel.

Gokturk, Sadik (1967). "Indivisibilities and Joint Production Under Perfect Competition: Toward a More General Theory of Production and Consumption." Unpublished paper, Columbia University (May 1967).

Hadley, G. (1964). *Nonlinear and Dynamic Programming*. Reading, Mass.: Addison-Wesley.

Haldi, J., and D. K. Whitcomb (1967). "Economies of Scale in Industrial Plants," *Journal of Political Economy*, Vol. 75 (August 1967), pp. 373–385.

Henderson, J. M., and R. E. Quandt (1958). *Microeconomic Theory—A Mathematical Approach*. New York: McGraw-Hill.

Henderson, John S. (1953). "Marginal Productivity Analysis—A Defect and a Remedy," *Econometrica*, Vol. 21 (January 1953), pp. 155–168.

Hicks, J. R. (1946). *Value and Capital*. 2d ed. Oxford: Clarendon Press.

Hirshleifer, J. (1956). "On the Economics of Transfer Pricing," *Journal of Business* (July 1956).

Karlin, Samuel (1959). *Mathematical Methods in Games, Programming and Economics—Volume II, The Theory of Infinite Games*. Reading, Mass.: Addison-Wesley.

Lancaster, K., and R. G. Lipsey (1956–57). "The General Theory of Second Best," *Review of Economic Studies*, Vol. XXIV, No. 63 (1956–57), pp. 11–33.

Lange, Oscar (1942). "The Foundations of Welfare Economics," *Econometrica*, Vol. 10, Nos. 3 and 4 (July–October 1942), pp. 215–228.

Luce, R. D., and H. Raiffa (1957). *Games and Decisions*. New York: Wiley.

McFadden, Daniel (1969). "A Simple Remark on the Second Best Optimality of Market Equilibria," *Journal of Economic Theory*, Vol. 1 (June 1969), pp. 26–38.

McManus, M. (1967). "Private and Social Costs in the Theory of Second Best," *Review of Economic Studies*, Vol. XXXIV, No. 99 (July 1967).

Meade, J. E. (1952). "External Economies and Diseconomies in a Competitive Situation," *Economic Journal* (March 1952).

Mishan, E. J. (1969). "The Relationship Between Joint Products, Collective Goods, and External Effects," *Journal of Political Economy* (May–June 1969), pp. 329–348.

—— (1971). "The Postwar Literature on Externalities: An Interpretative Essay," *Journal of Economic Literature*, Vol. IX, No. 1 (March 1971), pp. 1–28.

Pigou, A. C. (1932). *The Economics of Welfare*. 4th ed. New York: Macmillan (reprinted, 1952).

—— (1947). *A Study in Public Finance*. 3d ed. New York: Macmillan (reprinted, 1962).

Samuelson, P. A. (1947). *Foundations of Economic Analysis*. Cambridge, Mass.: Harvard University Press (reprinted, Atheneum, 1965).

—— (1954). "The Pure Theory of Public Expenditure," *Review of Economics and Statistics*, Vol. 36 (November 1954), pp. 387–389.

—— (1955). "Diagrammatic Exposition of a Theory of Public Expenditure," *Review of Economics and Statistics*, Vol. 37 (November 1955), pp. 350–356.

Shapley, L. S., and M. Shubik (1969). "On the Core of an Economic System with Externalities," *American Economic Review*, Vol. LIX, No. 4 (September 1969), pp. 678–684.

Shoup, C. S. (1965). "Public Goods and Joint Production," *Rivista Internazionale di Scienze Economiche e Commerciale*, Vol. 12 (March 1965), pp. 254–264.

Taylor, Angus E. (1955). *Advanced Calculus*. Boston: Ginn and Co.

Turvey, Ralph (1963). "On Divergences between Social Cost and Private Cost," *Economica* (August 1963), pp. 309–313.

Wellisz, S. (1964). "On External Diseconomies and the Government-Assisted Invisible Hand," *Economica* (November 1964), pp. 345–362.

Whinston, A. B. (1962). *Price Coordination in Decentralized Systems*. Ph.D. thesis, Carnegie Institute of Technology, O.N.R. Research Memorandum 99 (June 1962).

INDEX